Raw
and
Reverent

Studying Jesus' Powerful Prayer Life

Book One in the Women Treading Wisdom Series

Sandi Brandon

innovo
PUBLISHING

Published by
Innovo Publishing, LLC
www.innovopublishing.com
1-888-546-2111

innovo
PUBLISHING

Providing Full-Service Publishing Services for
Christian Authors, Artists & Organizations: Hardbacks, Paperbacks,
eBooks, Audiobooks, Music & Film

RAW AND REVERENT: STUDYING JESUS' POWERFUL PRAYER LIFE
BOOK ONE IN THE WOMEN TREADING WISDOM SERIES
Copyright © 2016 Sandi Brandon
All rights reserved.

Library of Congress Control Number: 2016947872
ISBN: 978-1-61314-315-5

Cover Design & Interior Layout: Innovo Publishing, LLC

Printed in the United States of America
U.S. Printing History
First Edition: September 2016

Foreword

Sandi Brandon is one of the elite prayer warriors of our time. She has developed a discipline through years of consistent prayer. What started out as a challenge from an older, wiser woman to work in a prayer room when Sandi was a young girl has become a passion that is evident to all who hear her pray.

Sandi's passionate prayers always leave people wishing they could pray like she does. Everyone desires to know what makes her prayers so beautiful. We wonder how she can close her eyes and pray with the words we wish we could say.

The compliments would often make Sandi giggle as she pondered the many hours she spent with our heavenly Father sharpening her focus on scripture and understanding the most amazing way to communicate with our Lord—prayer.

After numerous comments from people wishing they could have the ability to pray in the manner Sandi does, the women's ministry director at church asked her to write this wonderful Bible study. She has taken the mystery out of prayer and given us a solid foundation to build our relationship with the Lord.

If your prayer life isn't as disciplined as you'd like it to be or even if you'd like to just be comfortable praying in front of others, then this is the study for you. You may start this study as a kitty but I promise you will come out a lion!

Enjoy my special friend Sandi and all she has put into this study. She is an amazing teacher—the best kind of teacher—one who speaks from a position of knowledge from years and years of study and discipline.

PS—please know she has already been praying for you!

Jennifer Kruse
Christian speaker, writer
Sisterchat.wordpress.com

Contents

Preface

Why Raw and Reverent?

Why in the world would I pick the word *raw*? Two of my favorite people hate the word. For one of them, red, bloody ground beef creates unpleasant images in her head. For my other friend it elicits thoughts of intense, emotional pain causing her to grimace and shake her head. No doubt, your thoughts might turn to images of injured, exposed skin that feels every sensation. But God exposed the rawest pieces of my heart repeatedly through prayer. I will not pretend; sometimes it has been painful. But my sensitivity to the stimuli of God's whispers and work around me increases as I sit as His feet. Before investing time in prayer, consciousness of God's presence feels like a feather brushing our skin, possible to ignore. As we increase our time with Him, His nudge becomes something we recognize quicker. His hand feels familiar. Our awareness of His presence increases. I have had quite a few times during prayer that I felt like a four hundred-pound football player pushed me down a field against my planted heels, uprooting the grass and carrying me in a direction I did not want to go.

Reverent refers to an attitude of our hearts. When we truly recognize the magnitude of God we become still in wonder. Isaiah responded to seeing God with, "I am a man of unclean lips" (Isaiah 6:5), recognizing God Himself summons us to humility and awe. Though His holiness will rock our world, the best part is as we spend time with Him and His Word, not only do we understand more and more who He is, but we understand His character to see what He does for us: forgives us entirely, restores our soul, and blesses our lives.

As I set out to write a Bible study on prayer, I felt like Jesus had to set the foundation. God's Son established who we are, but Who could example prayer better? He gave us the Lord's Prayer, but He gave us so many more teachings and behaviors. So this study takes you through Luke to study those practices and determine how we set our foundation of prayer.

Note to the Reader

Hey, All!

I am so excited that you are joining us. My prayer is that you and I would walk away with a greater passion for knowing our star-breathing God through prayer.

After years of leading prayer teams for conferences, my women's ministry director asked me to teach prayer. Seeing God move through this amazing discipline sparks my teaching heart for you. As you begin this study, I know some days *seem* unrelated to prayer. Know that my intention is to help us weed out obstacles to prayer by looking at Jesus' example.

This study is set up with four days of homework each week. The intention is for you to keep weekends free to focus on your pastor's teaching, family time, and serving your own church. The day you meet for the study also has no homework. You can read through each day quickly or invest a little more by meditating on the memory verse with God.

Memory Verse: I believe in hiding God's Word in your heart, and each week gives you an option to supplement this study with memorization. If you don't want to memorize, my suggestion would be to spend time thinking about how it applies to your life and ask God if or how you could put it into practice better.

Nerd Alert: When you see these words, I have added a related topic that might clarify or supplement for those of us who love a little extra information. Annoyingly into details, my friends testify to my long-winded storytelling! If you find digging deeper interesting, you might enjoy these sections.

Verses are quoted in the English Standard Version of the Bible, unless otherwise specified. Feel free to use a different version if you prefer. Since this is a prayer study, I have started each day with a brief one-sentence prayer. Please engage God with these words or your own words before poring over the Bible text. I personally find scripture reading significantly more powerful when I am aware of the Spirit of God.

For the context of our study, prayer is defined as our conscious connection to God whether expressed in words, experience, or mental awareness. I will spare you the Greek details of why I went this direction. You're welcome.

Enjoy this time with God!

Sandi

Week One:
The Practice of Prayer

Teaching Session One: It Started with Him!

Prayer is _____ with God expressed by conscious _____ shared, asking, _____, and or _____.

1. RELATIONSHIP to God:
    Communication is where _____
    expresses itself.

    Prayer is not the _____ we do for God, or the
    _____ of Him, but it is where we meet Him
    _____.

    Our relationship _____ with _____!
    References: 1 John 4:10; John 3:16; Romans 5:8–10

2. Jesus' death unleashes God's _____ to _____ and me.

3. Three things to remember before starting this journey of prayer:
    All of us make _____.

    God initiated your _____.

    God _____ you.

4. God's story is bigger than your _____, bigger than
    your _____, bigger than your _____ and _____,
    and bigger than _____.

5. If we do not grasp that we are _____ and
    _____, our communication with God becomes about
    _____.

6. Our ability to talk to God was accomplished by _____. We did and can do _____ to earn that privilege.

7. Remember prayer is a _____.

What is our responsibility in prayer? _____
1 Thessalonians 5:17; Psalm 46:10a

Memory Verse

"Let us therefore come boldly unto the throne of grace, that we may obtain mercy, and find grace to help in time of need" (Hebrews 4:16, KJV).

Write out this verse in the translation of your choice:

Take a deep breath and repeat these words in your head or out loud.

What stands out in your heart and mind about your life regarding these words?

Week One, Day One:

Heart Obstacles, Anyone?

After today, each day's study will begin with a simple sentence to pray. Today, please allow me to say a prayer for you. Though it may feel strange, let's remember we serve a mighty God who can meet us right where we are, and I am trusting our star-breathing God to know my heart and more importantly to know *your* heart and *your* needs.

Our Amazing Father,

I pray, right now, for the heart and soul of this beautiful woman. I pray for Your Word to be anointed through this study in her life. I pray that You would work in her heart in every way she needs through these next weeks. Father, You know her. You know the needs. You know the wounds. You know the strengths. You know the gifting. You know what untruths need to be revealed to help her function fully as You intend. I pray that whatever You are working to accomplish would be accomplished. Use this study to participate in Your overriding plan in her life, Lord.

May her love for You increase. May her love for others increase. May her time with You in prayer reflect this increase. She is Your beautiful creation. Heal her wounds. Empower her strengths. Allow her to flourish in every way You intend.

I know well that You are the One who changes lives. You are the joy giver. You are the One who makes beauty from ashes. You are Healer of our souls. You are our Teacher and our friend. You are the One who redeems our lives from the pit by the power of Your Son submitting to death on a cross. I pray that at the end of this study, I wouldn't be noticed, but You will have rocked every piece of her world by Your beauty and might. I pray that Your Holy Spirit would be revealed.

I pray that the grace of Christ would have enveloped her heart. May she know You better than before.

I love and adore You. Help me to love and adore You more. I am 4everNawe[1] of You! Thank You beforehand for what You are going to do! Amen.

If you could see me after that prayer, you would see my tears. I am definitely raw and reverent at the thought of our amazing God at work in and through you.

Time on our knees accomplishes many things. No monk's tunic appears. No hair loss comes. No halo grows on our head. No perfection is attained. But prayer renders us more *raw* and more *reverent* indeed.

As we are all unique, our beliefs and desires about prayer vary. Some of us want a genie God to poof our every whim and wish the moment we speak, and that is how we treat prayer. But after talking to people all over this beautiful country of ours, I have learned that many of us are not that way at all. I have heard people say:

"God has a plan; He will implement it anyway, so why should I pray about it?"
"God shouldn't spend His time meeting my need; He has better things to do."
"I will do what I am supposed to do. I don't need outside help."
"I talk to God when things go well, because that's when my attitude is right."

Or I hear the other extreme:

"It is God's intention for me to be healthy and rich; I'm going to ask for it until He gives it to me."
"If you don't ask for the BMW, you are not having enough faith; just ask and believe. I am asking for exactly what I want, whatever it is!"

Some of us need to increase our faith and truly understand God oftentimes changes things when we pray. He will change your heart, but He will change much more than that! I heard a preacher from Africa in our country say, "I just don't understand American believers. In Africa, we are seeing God do miraculous wonders, but American believers don't seem to understand the power they have." I wanted to cower behind the person in front of me. Then some of us who are strong in faith need to stop acting like God's primary job is to fill our bank accounts and heal every sickness on demand. If we were God, we would have the power to make those decisions. We are not God, and trust me, we don't want that power. But I want to live in His power! I want to change lives in His power! I want to see His healing. Don't you? So let's set out together on this journey to learn how through prayer we can walk in Holy Spirit power, strength, and courage and see authentic change in our lives.

---

1   This is the author's website as well as her personal tag line. She often includes it in prayers she sends to people.

Our first step to becoming powerful pray-ers we talked about in the teaching session this week. We reviewed the miraculous intersection of humanity brought to God by way of Jesus on the cross. We, humans, destroy things and we build things, but our humanity is ever present. Yet God gifted us with the privilege of doing life with Him, the star breather. Why? Why do we get to talk to God? Why do we get to listen to God? Why do you think the Bible talks so much about prayer? Do you think prayer is just a way to pass the time? Does God just want to hear our useless banter about life? God loves you and me, so much that He allowed His Son to die so that we could have a relationship with Him. So, "Let us therefore **come boldly** unto the throne of grace, that we may obtain mercy, and **find grace to help** in time of need" (Hebrews 4:16, KJV, emphasis added).

Reviewing the teaching session this week, do you personally approach God with boldness? Why or why not?

Did you absorb into your soul the good news that God's Holy Spirit was unleashed as the veil tore from top to bottom **for you** and I to experience knowing God and walking in His presence and power? Whether you have never been a pray-er and are scared out of your mind, or if you have been walking with God for eighty years, I pray that God sets your heart ablaze afresh with the power that comes from walking with Him in prayer!

Let's review our mantra for this study as we close today:
God gave me the privilege of prayer.
I pray to participate with Him.
I battle in prayer.
I cry out by prayer.
God empowers me and changes things through my prayer.

Tomorrow, we jump in with both feet to trace Jesus' example of prayer in Luke. But I want you to think through your personal heart obstacles to why you hesitate to come to God even if it is as simple as mismanagement of time. Journal right now to God your struggle(s) about prayer. Ask God to open your eyes to the realities of His power. Ask Him to help you grasp whatever truth you need to become a power pray-er.

Week One, Day Two:

Why Do I Need Habits of Prayer?

Father, may I understand my own need to spend more time with You as I see Jesus' example.

From the teaching session this week and yesterday, I hope you have a firm grasp that you do not have to earn the right to come to God. Jesus did that for you.

Yesterday we talked about why you do or don't pray. Today, let's think about what your habits look like. Remember rules 1, 2, and 3—NO GUILT ALLOWED!

Here are some questions:

- How often do you pray and how would you describe your current prayer life?

- Do you even believe, really, that you should pray?

- Why or why not?

- How much time do you spend in prayer?

- Do you pray little, quick prayers throughout the day?

- Do you have a specific time to pray or specific place?

- Do you tend to pray more during crisis or good times?

- What types of things do you ask for from God?

- Do you go for long periods without praying at all?

- Do you devote any prayer time to recognizing His characteristics? How often do you thank Him?

- Do you devote any time to listening to Him?

- Do you pray about spiritual growth?
- Do you speak in specifics in your requests and conversation with God or do you generalize?
- Do you pray as you read scripture?
- Do you journal?
- Do you ask for things over and over that you want or tend to not ask at all?

Just think about this last question, we will revisit it after you look at Jesus' habits. How do you desire your time spent in prayer to look different after this study?

If you want to follow Christ, but really don't think prayer is necessary, I hope seeing His example will change your mind. So as we turn the corner to look at Jesus' example of prayer. Let's walk with Jesus through His words and practice in the book of Luke. Forgive me if I stretch you as we jump in with both feet. Reviewing each time Jesus prays, we are skipping much of Luke to maintain a clear focus on prayer.

Please read through Jesus' practice and teaching of prayer in Luke:

3:21–22
4:1–2
5:15–16
6:12–13
9:18, 28–36
10:21–22
11:1–4, 8–10
22:31–32, 39–46
23:34, 44–46

If Jesus, with God's genes on earth (fully human as well, Hebrews 4) needed to retreat so often in just a three-year ministry, how much more do we need to follow His example? Our gifting and accomplishments can lead us to think we don't need time with God. Productivity can downright deceive us into thinking we are accomplishing more without prayer. Why waste God's time or ours when we can be producing results? Jesus didn't seem to feel that way, Friends. Just because you are clear on His mission for your life does not mean you are excluded from needing His direction, empowerment, and participation.

Some of the things you read in these passages create a pretty clear picture of how much Jesus included the Father in His everyday life. We see Jesus in a regular practice of retreating from the crowd, even to pray and meditate all night. We see Jesus prepare and fight temptation with fasting and prayer. We see Jesus consult God just before making a big decision: choosing disciples. We see Jesus pray for Peter and even the people who were persecuting Him. We see Jesus consult God and big things happen like the heavens splitting open and the Holy Spirit falling in the form of a dove, clouds swirling with the transfiguration and faces turning white, soldiers storming in to make the arrest. We see Jesus beg for a change of circumstance.

Over the next weeks we will cover this list, so be mindful of preparing your heart as you review them.

- Everyday practice of retreating and meditating
- Dealing with temptation/spiritual warfare by prayer and fasting
- Consulting God for a big decision
- Praying for Himself and those around Him
- Crying out for a change of circumstance
- Calling on God for miraculous results

In which of these practices is it easier for you to include God?

Which of these practices challenge you the most?

Let's revisit this question now that we have looked at Jesus' example. After this study, how do you want your prayer time to look different?

Take a moment to talk to God about this study and pray for your own growth in prayer over the next few weeks.

Week One, Day Three:

Should I Ask Again and Again?

Father, help me to understand how to plead earnestly and persistently for Your heart's desire.

Yesterday, we talked about the things we saw Jesus do, and we will be covering these over the next few weeks:

- Everyday practice of retreating and meditating
- Dealing with temptation by prayer and fasting
- Consulting God for a big decision
- Praying for those around Him
- Crying out for a change of circumstance
- Calling on God for miraculous results

So we looked at Jesus' example, and hopefully we evaluated our current personal habits. I know those questions might have stepped into your personal space. But my prayer is God will step into our personal space. Jesus is going to teach us a story about something I hear women feel guilty about all the time: repeating a request in prayer. It's almost like they want to apologize for asking God again. I hear:

"Well, I already asked God and I didn't get an answer so I assume it is a no."

"I am not believing God heard me if I ask Him again for that."

"God knows what is best; I don't need to ask."

"God is sovereign and is making the decision; I don't need to ask."

Today we are going to read a couple of parables Jesus shared about repeating the same request to God. Have you ever felt like it might annoy God if you asked over and over? Or worse, repeating a request to God, you felt like you were not trusting Him or exercising enough faith. Read what Jesus had to say about this in Luke 18:1–7.

1. What did Luke say at the end of verse one about what point Jesus was making?

Just for fun, let's look at this phrase in a few different versions.
NIV—"always pray and not give up."
The Message—"pray consistently and never give up."
ESV—"always pray and not lose heart."

2. So Jesus clearly wanted His disciples to stick to prayer and asking. What does this tell you about your practice or hesitance to ask God repeatedly?

Now read Luke 11:5–13. Jesus addresses this same concept from a little different angle.
3. Whatever you are asking for, is God going to give you something that would harm you? What does verse 12 say about that?

4. What specific requests have you repeatedly asked of God?

5. Do you ever feel stuck in a loop repeating the same scene over and over in your prayer life? What kind of things did you stop asking because God had not given it to you yet?

Let's read James 4:2–3.
6. What does the end of verse 2 say about why you don't have?

7. What reason does verse 3 give that God may not grant a request?

8. How does your personal request from question 4 fit with this parameter?

Before we complete today's lesson, let's review one other important piece of persisting in prayer. Part of this passage is so familiar, but let's look at it in its full context. Here is Jeremiah 29:10–14:

> For thus says the Lord: "When seventy years are completed for Babylon, I will visit you, and I will fulfill to you my promise and bring you back to this place. For I know the plans I have for you, declares the Lord, plans for welfare and not for evil, to give you a future and a hope. Then you will call upon me and come and pray to me, and I will hear you. **You will seek me and find me, when you seek me with all your heart.** I will be found by you, declares the Lord, and I will restore your fortunes and gather you from all the nations and all the places where I have driven you, declares the Lord, and I will bring you back to the place from which I sent you into exile." (emphasis added)

Now let's go back to Jesus' words from earlier today in Luke 11:10: "For everyone who asks receives, and the one who seeks finds, and to the one who knocks it will be opened."

As God spoke these powerful words in Jeremiah about giving a future and a hope, it began with a seventy-year, God-caused exile according to His own words in verse 14. Have you felt like you were in a God-caused exile? Don't give up hope, Friend. You have a future and a hope. But also don't miss your responsibility: "Then you will **call upon me** and come and **pray** to me, and I will hear you. **You will seek me and find me, when you seek me with all your heart**" (Jeremiah 29:12–14, emphasis added). Our soul yearns for the treasure of God and verbalizes that heart desire by praying. Let's trust God will "restore our fortunes" and "return us" from exile.

When I started begging God for a neighbor and family friend's salvation, I was a teenage girl with a crush on his son. Important tasks filled my calendar like crafting two foot-wide, and tall, hair with Aqua Net, a curling iron, and Scrunchies. Bon Jovi, Def Leppard, and Boston blared from my radio as I darted through the neighborhood. I may still dart around town, but thirty years of straight hair later, my teenagers have their own crushes. My daughter straightens her curly locks. I can honestly say praying continued diligently for our neighbor and family friend. When the phone call came that God had granted that request, it should not have surprised me. I could lie to you and say, "Of course, I knew he would accept Jesus!" But the truth is, upon hearing the news, on my couch, I sat stunned, rocked to my foundations by our amazing God. Over thirty years, countless requests flooded God's ears. God knew. Thank You, Lord!

Do you want to heed James' warning with me? I don't want to not have, because I didn't ask. I want many things for my husband and children. I want to be a better parent and friend. I want more people to know Him. I want God to be moving and changing lives! I want to know Him more myself! Let's make sure we seek to find every treasure God wants to give us and ASK!

So, what is it you need to keep asking?

Week One, Day Four:
The Bad News and the Good News

Father, give me a heart to know You will meet me if I continue in prayer.

Charles Stanley, well-known pastor, writer, and teacher says this, "The amount of time we spend with Jesus— meditating on His Word and His majesty, seeking His face—establishes our fruitfulness in the kingdom."[2]

So far this week, we thought through what keeps us personally from praying more, why we should make a habit of prayer by reviewing Jesus' practice of prayer, and reviewed some of His teachings about committing to pray hard and ask often. Today, there is good news and bad news. The bad news is maturity in prayer comes the same way other maturity comes—with time and practice. The good news is if we choose to make the commitment, God will empower you and mature you in ways you have only dreamed!

Let's talk about the bad news first. Growing up in prayer means making a decision to exercise discipline and commit to creating these habits of praying in your life. I don't think I am the only impatient, results-oriented person. My human system to master something quickly means pursuing it quickly and passionately. I will read every book I can find about the topic, educate myself, Google as much information as I can find, find people with experience, then proclaim myself proficient. How many sayings do we have about patience in accomplishing important things? Progress, not perfection. It is a journey, not a destination. A marathon, not a sprint. Understand, Friend, maturity in prayer will not come in record-setting time. Whether you have been doing this journey with Him for six months or sixty years, it is a process.

For our example, once again let's start with Jesus. At twelve years old, our young Lord deliberated in conversation with the synagogue leaders, yet His

---

2   Brainy Quote, Charles Stanley, http://www.brainyquote.com/quotes/quotes/c/charless-ta181232.html

ministry did not begin until He was thirty years old! Jesus, God's genes on earth, took eighteen years to come out to the world as the Son of God! (If you want to read this timeline, see Luke 2:41–52, and Luke 3:21–23.) Imagine Jesus studying, memorizing Old Testament texts, and praying. Eighteen years went by. "And Jesus increased in wisdom and in stature and in favor with God and man" (Luke 2:52).

Wisdom came even to the Son of God with years. Shouldn't you give yourself a little grace for the process?

Recently, a dear friend desperately needed her circumstances to change. Every fiber of my being wanted to pull her out. I didn't want her to have to wait for circumstances to improve. I didn't want her process to be so hard. While writing this, I flew from Memphis, Tennessee, to Phoenix, Arizona, in less than three hours. These days, we can do almost anything immediately and with ease. I like quick and immediate so much that I have speeding tickets in eleven states, and I am sure every one of those tickets were the result of me wanting to accomplish something faster. But God's time table is not our time table. Some pieces God will put together quickly; others He will not. I told you yesterday I prayed for thirty years for someone's salvation. Abraham and Sarah waited until their nineties to see God's promise of a child. The Israelites were in slavery in Egypt for four hundred years. The Messiah came after four hundred years of silence. Even Jesus waited eighteen years to minister.

Let God manage the timing. You get down and get dirty committing to pray for things that matter.

Now let's get to the good news; it is actually great news. If you make this commitment to become a pray-er and you obey God, Precious One, your spiritual growth and spiritual eyes will revolutionize your relationship and experience with God. Many of us are committed to Bible study, or committed to a particular ministry, but if you commit to pray with just that mustard seed of believing God, combining it with Bible study and obedience, God will rock your foundation! When you start growing up in prayer, you become a person who has an awareness of where God is at work. One of my favorite things is when I am with a group who is praying and my mind is saying the words or concepts that are coming out of someone else's mouth. It is so much fun to see the Holy Spirit directing a group to pray for something specific. You will gain an unexplained awareness of where God is moving. Your pastor's sermons might move you to act quicker. The words "the power of prayer" we hear so often came from believer's who witnessed that power. I have seen people healed. I have experienced God do the miraculous. But my favorite part is being blessed to see God at work in the simple and the mundane. What could be more beautiful than being a person who notices God making beauty from ashes in the ups and downs of every day?

This is the reward. Yes, I am not going to lie, it's a commitment. It is a spiritual discipline. God gifted us with salvation, and all we have to do is recognize and accept it. God also gifted us with prayer, and all we have to do is exercise it! Choose to pray. You will not regret it.

With all we have looked at this week about your hesitations and habits, Jesus' practice and teaching, where does your heart land right now?

Are you willing to ask God to help you commit to becoming a woman of prayer?

If that one makes you uncomfortable, can I ask that you commit to finish this study? You have already made it through the first week if you are here!

"Even youths shall faint and be weary, and young men shall fall exhausted; but they who wait for the Lord shall renew their strength; they shall mount up with wings like eagles; they shall run and not be weary; they shall walk and not faint" (Isaiah 40:30–31).

Product Pushing another Time Taker? The Habit of Journaling...

Throughout this study, specific heart thoughts will be put to paper. It takes more time, but I believe in writing or typing things out. For me, it slows and focuses my flighty brain. Where my teens need to be, the job I need to complete, and that stuff sitting on the kitchen counter become less prominent when I am actively writing my prayer. Other perks come with journaling. Seeing your prayers answered on paper confirms your belief. You record the deepest of your heart's convictions. That tangible record helps you remember what you were hearing from God. If you don't want to be a person who journals, I understand. But I ask you to consider during this study, physically writing out your prayers and thoughts. It is a discipline that can dramatically affect our prayer journey. A dear friend resisted journaling for many years, but when she did a prayer study that required it, her passion for prayer multiplied. Putting her thoughts on paper yielded results. I know it takes time, but for this study please consider practicing journaling alongside prayer.

Nerd Alert

The Greek word for prayer is *proseuche* (pros-yoo-khay).

Pros by itself means "at, near, by" or "to, towards." *Euche* means "prayer to God" or "vow." The word in its entirety can even mean a place that is used for communication with God. Often, it denotes a place with water that is used to clean the hands before prayer is offered.

Focus on *at, near, by,* or *towards* to include anytime you are aware of God's presence.

Week Two:
Not My Will, But Thine

Teaching Session Two:
When to Exercise Faith and When to Surrender

Remember the different answers to prayer.

- (2 Samuel 12:15–22, David's son)

- (Jonah 3:5–10)

- (Birth of Sarah's baby Isaac and Messiah's coming)

Why No's?
So that God can be glorified.
Because God sees and knows all the factors.
Because of free will.
Because it is actually what's best for you.

1. Watch out for _____! The pitfall of the pity party can _____ you of today's _____ and _____.

2. Jesus taught on believing God to do the miraculous, and He said, "Not my will, but thine." I want to _____ on the side of _____, but I have to _____ Him.

3. Never assume that prayer will put us above the _____ of God or that_____ will not exist in your life because you pray. Hebrews 12:5–7.

SIDE NOTE: How do you know if you or the person you are listening to are on target?

Are you or the teacher in any way _____ Jesus? 2 Peter 2:1–2

Are you or the teacher implying that _____ will happen?
Micah 2:6–7; John 16:33

Are your or your teacher's conclusions originating from _____ and
_____?

1 Timothy 6:3

Are you or your teacher enjoying taking strong stances in
_____? 1 Timothy 6:3–4

An argumentative spirit leads to _____, _____, _____ and
_____.

GOOD NEWS: Remember, God knows what is best and is looking out for you!

Memory Verse

saying, "Father, if you are willing, remove this cup from me. Nevertheless, not my will, but yours, be done" (Luke 22:42).

Write out this verse in the translation of your choice:

Week Two, Day One:
Surrendering Your Plans

*Lord, teach me how I can pray believing, and still understand it is Your will
that needs to be done.*

Are you old enough or been in church long enough to remember the old
hymn, "Have Thine Own Way, Lord"? The lyrics were so powerful. If you know
the melody, sing to your heart's content:

"Have thine own way, Lord!
Have thine own way!
Thou art the potter, I am the clay.
Mold me and make me after thy will,
While I am waiting, yielded and still."[3]

Does your heart align with these words? These words remind me of what
we are talking about today. Jesus' prayed words "Not my will, but thine," do
those words resonate anything in your heart? Are they just words you heard in
church? Are they words you don't want to think about because you really want
God to do what *you* desire, not the other way around?

Read through Luke 22:39–44. Jesus is about to be arrested, put through
trial after trial, ultimately ending with Him nailed to a cross.

So what cup was Jesus asking to pass?

---

3   Hymn "Have Thine Own Way, Lord" written by Adelaide A. Pollard. Music by George C.
     Stebbins. 1906. Public domain.

What did he say to close verse 42? (Hint: Look back a page, or at the title of this chapter.)

Do you struggle with what "after thy will" means when it comes to prayer? How do we ask God for what we want and at the same time, genuinely mean "not my will, but thine"? Jesus provides an example of this for us. He spills His heart's desire to not go to the cross, but this particular time, even the very thing Jesus desired was ultimately not the Father's will.

I don't want to ever presume the mind or plans of God, so I recognize this story is told through my eyes. Maybe you will relate to this prayer story. My heartfelt prayers cover no one more often or sincerely than my children. Yet significant challenges seem to follow my thirteen-year-old. Okay, the challenges have not been hunger or lack of American comforts. She has had the creature comforts so many of us Americans have. However, three long-distance moves have wreaked emotional havoc. Dyslexia brought inabilities to write, feelings of stupidity, and experience in rejection by other students. Four concussions meant losing her favorite thing to do—soccer. She has repeatedly been rejected by friends. Now, maybe sometimes her painful truth telling might have been the cause. (I don't know where she gets that from!) But it seems like there are always obstacles for her to overcome. The other day another one of these obstacles showed up, and I asked, "Honey, when these things happen, do you ever feel like God is against you?" She responded, "Mom, for a long time I thought that. I was mad at Him. Now, I understand that God has given me those challenges to make me a better person. And He has given me friends, a great family, and an amazing place to live. What do I really have to be mad at Him about?" WARNING: Proud Mama alert! Yes, I was beaming. But can I tell you that the hours I have prayed for that child, I never once asked for dyslexia, concussions, or heartbreak. I asked for her character. I asked for her to love God. Honestly, would I have asked for character if I thought the answer would be dyslexia, concussions, and social issues? I don't know. My plans did not happen. My will would have been for her to have comfort, comfort, and more comfort. And for God to magically tap her shoulder with His wand to grant her love for Him. I wanted to rub the God genie bottle, and poof! But my desire for her ease of life was not to be.

Have you had plans that went different from what you prayed?

Do you have stories like the one I described? Maybe the experience was difficult, but the results were better than you could have anticipated? Would you list it here?

Balancing two opposing things can be hard. So I believe, ask, and know God can heal Anna's dyslexia, but I also acknowledge His plans might include dyslexia. Praying boldly for healing of that dyslexia, which I do want for my child, stopped at some point along the way. Instead, now I ask for Him to be glorified in and through it. I ask for her to learn from it. I ask for her dyslexia to provide opportunities for growth and ministry. I have surrendered my plans for her life to His greater plan, trusting Him. My prayer changed instead of the circumstance.

Read 2 Corinthians 12:7–10. What did Paul ask for?

How many times did he ask?

What does the first few words of verse 9 tell you about Paul's attitude?

When you don't get what you ask for, how do you respond?

Do you doubt God, fight God, or surrender to His decision with gladness?

Whatever your answer, think of times you have done this the way Paul did, and times you have not. What do you think made the difference?

Journal a prayer about surrendering your plans to God's wisdom.

Week Two, Day Two:
Surrendering Your Fears

Father, teach me what "not my will, but thine" means as I release my worries and fears to You.

Fear. What comes to your mind when we say the word *fear*? How does fear affect the way or time you talk to God? My dad teases that an atheist on his deathbed quickly becomes a desperate praying believer. For instance, if I were standing at the top of a cliff ready to bungee jump, my prayer discussion would look much different than if I were facing an underlying fear that my child's success would ever come. Yesterday, we saw how Jesus feared going to the cross, and He released that fear to God, and followed God's will instead of His own.

So let's think about our fears and worries. Knotted so tightly together, I prefer not to separate these two things. Worry often originates in some fear. Worry is fear's practice ground inside our head. I have a fear of snakes. Living in Arizona, when I hike in all our beautiful parks, that imagined rattlesnake hiding under every rock is me allowing fear to make my mind its worry playground. But the fears that might grip me usually surround the people I care about.

What are the fears that plague your mind?

What do you habitually worry about?

Moses worried he wasn't articulate enough to lead Israel. Esther chose to overcome her fear and approach a king who could kill her for doing so. Jonah

37

feared of all things that Nineveh would repent and God would forgive them. So there are fears, good and bad, in our lives as well, right? We have fears when we represent God too, don't we? What fears or worries have you had regarding something spiritual you wanted to do or felt prompted to do?

Parenting is a God-given assignment. If you are a parent, you know parenting and worry feel like they are knotted together with super glue! My worst screeching-shrew-psycho Mom spills out when there is underlying fear. No wonder "Do not fear" repeats throughout scripture. Attending Moms in Prayer groups all over this country, I have prayed with many moms. Inevitably, prayer ends with someone loudly sighing relief. All laugh. After those minutes of prayer, we physically feel relief from releasing fear and worry to God.

Read Philippians 4:6–7. What does it say will happen when you make your requests known to God?

Have you experienced a peace that surpasses all understanding? The Message is another paraphrase of the scripture from Hebrew and Greek by longtime pastor, Eugene Peterson. I will probably mention this concept a few times because I love his words in James about prayer:

> If you don't know what you're doing, pray to the Father. He loves to help, and won't be condescended to when you ask for it. Ask boldly, believingly, without a second thought. People who "worry their prayers" are like wind-whipped waves. Don't think you're going to get anything from the Master that way, adrift at sea, keeping all your options open. (James 1:5–8, The Message)

When I read these words, I realize I often "worry my prayers." How do you think you worry your prayers?

In the teaching session this week, we talked about how believing God will answer your prayer (faith) and asking boldly and repeatedly work together. In Week Two, Day One, we saw Paul asking for something God would not grant.

Instead of worrying our prayers, let's attempt to release our fears and worries to God right now in prayer. Sometimes when I release something to God, I will physically open my hands to God as a sign I am releasing my worry, fear, sin, or heart to Him. Journal your worries and specific fears for today to God here and now, then close your eyes and open your hands to Him, and sigh the relief from letting those things go.

Week Two, Day Three:

Surrendering Your Actions

Lord, help me to have the courage to obey what I hear in prayer, particularly when it's not my will.

We looked earlier this week at Jesus, begging for a different way other than going to the cross, but hours later, one step at a time, He obeyed and willingly suffered on that cross. Though our instructions are probably not as challenging as going to a cross, God might make something clear He is asking you to do.

Let's read through the burning bush conversation between Moses and God in Exodus 3:1–4:17.

What does the text say God heard in verse 7, and came to Him in verse 9? (The form of the word may vary depending on your translation.)

God's people "cry" out to Him, and God charges Moses as the cavalry to rescue them. God calls Moses to speak to Pharaoh. How did Moses feel about what God was asking him to do? (3:11, 13, 4:1, 10, 13)

What has God asked you to do?

In prayer, God might ask you to obey something that seems crazy. Many decades ago, one of my dearest friends betrayed me. I do not trust people easily, and the story could have been a made-for-TV drama. Implicitly trusting her, my heart was devastated. The type of devastation that after thirty years, nightmares occasionally awaken me reliving those weeks. Knowing God required us to forgive people; I knew forgiveness to be mandatory. So I decided to quietly dismiss the friendship and go on a "goodbye" trip to close that friendship chapter.

While praying and reading my Bible on the trip, I had an experience with God that felt like a conversation, not audible, but something I sensed: "Forgive her."

My response was, "I have forgiven her. I am here, aren't I?"

"Sandi, I am telling you to fully restore the relationship and offer genuine and complete grace, the same kind I offer you." I didn't think this was fair or realistic, and much too much to ask. We had been best friends, and the betrayal wound loomed large and fresh. Not only did I not want to obey—it nauseated and terrified me to let this person hold any position of close friendship—but God empowered me to do what He asked me to do. My friend and I spent days reviewing the reasons she made the choices she did, and we reviewed things I had done that could have contributed to her actions. Though we assessed the situation a little differently, God gave me the strength and understanding to obey Him. God restored the relationship. I am so thankful He pushed, and that I chose to obey. This person is still one of my best friends. I love her and her kids as if they were my own.

Responding to God's directives and surrendering our actions hurts sometimes. In prayer, His Word might leap off the page with how you are supposed to respond to a situation or tell you to obey something that feels like the opposite of rational behavior.

Jesus walked to a beating and allowed Himself to be crucified on a cross. Moses appeared before a Pharaoh.

Have you experienced knowing God's voice in prayer and knowing what He wanted you to do?

Since my story thirty years ago, there have been countless times I knew I was supposed to take a step of action. I won't even slightly imply I have obeyed perfectly, quickly, or particularly with the right attitude. What I will say is obeying God brings peace that truly goes beyond our comprehension. I never questioned forgiving my dear friend, and there has been tremendous blessing from a choice to release the relationship to God. She has been with me through the death of my brother, countless challenges, and I am so thankful I chose to hear and obey God. I don't think Jesus regrets walking to the cross to save all of humanity. And Moses' obedience resulted in the Israelites being freed from slavery. But there will be times you don't get to see a clear result like those, and we have to choose to act on what God asked us to do, and trust Him, that His plan and way is best.

Richard Foster in his book, *Prayer: Finding the Heart's True Home*[4] put it this way:

> Part of the answer lies in the fact that frequently we hold on so tightly to the good that we do know that we cannot receive the greater good that we do not know. God has to help us let go of our tiny vision in order to release the greater good he has in store for us.

Journal about any experience you have with surrendering to God's will in your action from your past.

Journal about any action or step you might need to take today.

---

4   Richard Foster, *Prayer: Finding the Heart's True Home* (New York: HarperCollins Publishers, 1982).

Week Two, Day Four:
Surrendering Your Heart

Father, as I pray, may my heart become more like Your heart for the people around me, as well as for Your larger purposes in the world. Teach me how to see Your will and follow You.

I married my handsome husband in 1996. Aside from not being bad on the eyes, he is kindhearted, hardworking, and crazy fun. Once we got married though, I learned there was much more to him than just those characteristics. I want life on a general schedule. I like to go to bed during a window of time between 9:30–10:30 p.m. He likes to go to bed between 1:00–2:00 a.m. I want to go out every Friday night, and prefer it to be around 5:30, so then if I want to go to a movie, I am not falling asleep. He would prefer to stay home and decompress from his week, with something cooked at home. I like to do my weekend's work Saturday morning, so I can relax the rest of the weekend. He wants to sleep Saturday morning, relax Saturday afternoon, and start the work between 4:00 p.m. and 5:00 p.m. working into the night. I am ready to play by Saturday afternoon. I want the TV off most of the time. He wants the TV on most of the time. Potential arguments could erupt over any of these preferences.

Guess what happened? We love each other. We learned each other's preferences, and we both find ways to compromise, so that we can be together on the weekend. I won't pretend there hasn't been some tension around these issues, but we love each other enough to figure it out. I stay up later at night, and he goes to bed earlier. As much as he hates me getting out of the bed early in the morning, he accepts that his wife won't be in the bed when he gets up most mornings. We stay home Friday night, but pick up food so I get to "go out." It starts anywhere between 6:30 or 7:00 p.m., which works for both of us. Of course, much more important things have also changed, because I want what is best for Bill. My heart pulls for things he wants that I never wanted before because I love him and vice versa.

We have a heart for each other, and therefore change happens in our attitudes and actions. Doesn't this same thing happen when we love God? As our passion grows for our God, our actions adjust to God's desires.

Read Psalm 37:4. What is the first phrase in this verse?

How does your "delight" come from the Lord?

If your delight does come from the Lord, what does the verse say will happen?

As you spend more time with God, your love for Him grows, and your actions change. Unlike Bill and me, God already knows what is best for you. As your heart becomes more for His heart, you will find your requests in prayer will change. For me personally, this change has been that when I pray for people, my focus centers more on their spiritual condition, and less on their comfort. I will still ask for healing, but I will be more focused on how God can be glorified in any given situation. I trust God's intentions and plans more than I did when our relationship was new; therefore, I ask for His intentions and plans.

Earlier this week, we saw Paul ask for his thorn to be removed, so we know he still prayed for himself and his desire. Now let's take a closer glance at Paul. Notice particularly how Paul's heart is centered around others and God instead of his comfort. Remember, Paul was in jail during much of this writing. For each of these passages, answer: 1) Who is Paul concerned about? 2) What is Paul's goal whether in prayer or just looking at the words?

Acts 25–26. Paul and Silas are jailed, and yet where is their focus?

Romans 1:8–11

Romans 15:5–6, 13

Ephesians 3:14–20

Philippians 3:8–11

Colossians 1:9–12

Any conclusions on who Paul's heart was for in prayer?

What can we learn from Paul?

We have talked about surrendering our plans, fears, actions, and heart in prayer this week. Surrender is never easy.

Week Three:
Spiritual Warfare

Teaching Session Three: Know the Obstacles

1. Obstacles from God
   God's plan is much better than your plan, and they probably differ.

2. Obstacles from Us
   Where is your heart? Do you take the time to evaluate it? James 4:3

   Have you honestly confessed your sin? Isaiah 59:2; Psalm 66:18

   Are you harboring any anger or unforgiveness? 1 Peter 3:7; Ephesians 5:22–24

   Do you believe and trust God to do it? James 1:5–8. Remember The Message?

   Are you taking God seriously? Ecclesiastes 5:1–7, Holy of Holies

3. Obstacles from the Enemy
   Are you aware and expecting the enemy's attacks?

   Recognize _____ fights the enemy more effectively than _____ can.

   - 2 Corinthians 3:5–6
   - The battle with the enemy happens
     _____.
   - Ephesians 6:13–20

Memory Verse

"For we do not wrestle against flesh and blood, but against the rulers, against the authorities, against the cosmic powers over this present darkness, against the spiritual forces of evil in the heavenly places" (Ephesians 6:12).

Write out this verse in the translation of your choice:

Week Three, Day One:
Understanding There Is an Enemy

Lord, show me the realities of my enemy and Yours.

Written to fulfill Jana's—my women's ministry director—request to teach prayer, my passion for prayer leapt onto these pages. Publishing a book, the dream of many, had never crossed my mind. The dream crossed my reality suddenly and unexpectedly.

For years, I blatantly warned fellow pray-ers how when prayer is involved, life tornadoes seem to appear from nothing. Now a publisher was involved in this prayer study, and guess what? In the first week, those tornadoes came. My thirteen-year-old experienced a life change about which I am sworn to secrecy. An epic extended-family fight occurred. My best friend's dad became incapacitated by a stroke. A college roommate's mom was diagnosed with cancer. Though more chaotic than tragic, the kids started back to school. But one more tragedy . . . the week ended with answering a phone call from the police to come immediately. I found myself holding my friend in a hospital room as the doctors delivered factual medical sentences. Those sentences conveyed that her handsome, muscular, forty-year-old husband had died from a heart attack. Hours later, I witnessed her delivering this shocking development that would forever change her precious children's futures. The beautiful, blonde eleven-year-old daughter, and witty, crystal blue-eyed thirteen-year-old boy regularly swam in my pool, played in my house, and now their dad, and our friend, was gone. My heart broke for them.

Was it just a coincidence, mathematical probability aside, for this many drastic events to all occur within five days of each other?

I don't believe so.

I know, it sounds crazy in a world where we only weigh events with mathematic probabilities and the current theories of science. Certainly, I am not saying the world was revolving around me. I don't think our friend died because I had written a book on prayer. I don't know how it all works together. God knows those specifics. But my experience with prayer predicts an unexpected arrival of tornadoes.

Jesus spent forty days in the wilderness praying and fasting, and guess who showed up? Jesus was actively praying, and stage right, the devil himself entered. Personally, if the devil showed up to whisk me through temptations, I might scream, "Tornado! Tornado! Tornado!"

If you want to become a person accomplishing big things in God's kingdom in prayer, expect these tornadoes. You will learn to push through them, and they will decrease in frequency if you persevere. But nausea, a flat tire, an argument, a rock in the windshield, or a crazy, random thought of temptation will arrive to derail you. I believe those distractions, somehow, are from who the Bible calls our enemy: Satan, or the devil. In spiritual circles and scripture, spiritual warfare is the term.

The devil showed up during Jesus' prayer time. Trust me, he or his minions will show up for yours. It might be before, during, or after prayer. It won't be every time. And they won't be dressed in a red cloak, red horns, and a pitchfork. At times, you will not recognize who or what it is.

Have you ever tried to accomplish something spiritual to find yourself in something like my description here? Have you ever attempted to join a prayer group or attend a prayer session to never find the opportunity or make it? Explain your experience with this.

Ponder this question: How does believing there is an enemy impact you each day?

If your truthful answer is, "It doesn't have any effect on my day," I ask you to consider the possibility. You are reading a book about prayer, so I respectfully ask you to pray and ask God to reveal to you what you need to know. Many of us believe there is an enemy, but we are living like he doesn't exist.

Do you really believe there is an enemy to your well-being, soul? How does this affect the way you pray?

How do you think it should affect the way you pray?

Job's story goes on for forty-two chapters, but let's read Job 1:6–22. What did you learn Satan does in verse 7?

What did you learn about God in:
    verse 8?

    verse 10?

    verse 12?

Now read 1 Peter 5:8–11. How does this relate?

We saw in the Old and New Testament that Satan was, and is, roaming the earth, looking to devour someone. Then in Job, we also saw that:

1. God pointed Job out to Satan.
2. God had been protecting Job.
3. God alone had the authority around Job's life.

In the next section, we will go through Jesus' temptation. Ask God any questions you have about spiritual warfare or your enemy, and journal your thoughts about these three points or the thoughts of an enemy here:

Nerd Alert

Praying Hedges

Playing football with the neighborhood boys, I fell into a holly bush hedge once. I would prefer to not repeat that moment in the cactus hedges around Arizona where I live now! In Bible times, people built plant hedges to keep out predators. Hedges costs significantly less than building a fence. As we walk through some scripture that mentions hedges, let's envision the security a hedge brings as well as the redirection that a hedge might cause. Even a hedge maze causes the person inside to take specific routes determined by where the hedges are located. Have you felt like you were walking a maze with life decisions? Did you ask yourself, "Which turn do I make next?" I have.

How does this relate to prayer? I often hear someone pray a hedge around another person. Where did this originate? Two specific hedges are mentioned in scripture. Hosea 2:6–7 says, "Therefore I will hedge up her way with thorns, and I will build a wall against her, so that she cannot find her paths. She shall pursue her lovers but not overtake them, and she shall seek them but shall not find them. Then she shall say, 'I will go and return to my first husband, for it was better for me then than now.'" You and I can pray that prayer for someone we love to get out of a specific bad behavior. In Job 1:10, Satan says to God about Job, "Have you not put a hedge around him and his house and all that he has, on every side? You have blessed the work of his hands, and his possessions have increased in the land." So Satan knew his authority was limited and Job was protected by God. Though Jesus doesn't use the word hedge in Luke 22:31–32a, Jesus said, "Simon, Simon, behold, Satan demanded to have you, that he might sift you like wheat, but I have prayed for you that your faith may not fail."

If you want someone's protection from the enemy, these prayers give us insight into how to pray for ourselves and others. Do you want God to hedge you in so your sin, or someone else's, is painful and helps you stay on course? Do you need the enemy kept at bay? I think we all need and desire God's protection He offered Job. I prefer evading Satan's sifting too, please!

Week Three, Day Two:
Praying Scripture, Jesus' Use of Scripture in Battle

Father, teach me to commit myself to knowing Your Word and how to pray it.

In Day One this week, we talked about how the enemy showing up can look like a tornado. Let's follow with how Jesus responded to the tornado of the devil. Read Luke 4:1–13.

What does Jesus respond with in verses 4, 8 and 10?

_____

We are going to spend time meditating on scripture on a different week. But this is a little different. Jesus addresses specific temptation and the enemy with scripture. Knowing scripture helps you combat false things, and I believe you will find that praying scripture brings power to fight these battles. We aren't addressing temptation specifically today, but we address praying scripture to combat the enemy.

Wherever you are in your prayer journey, you know at least a little scripture. Beth Moore and other authors devote entire books to praying scripture. My husband loves to pray the prayer of Jabez. I blanket my prayers in scripture, whether in exact phrases or concepts.

Just a little caution: remember Matthew 6:6–7:

But when you pray, go into your room and shut the door and pray to your Father who is in secret. And your Father who sees in secret will reward you. And when you pray, do not heap up empty phrases as the Gentiles do, for they think that they will be heard for their many words.

There is no "prayer formula." It is so easy for us to turn things into a list. I have made the mistake of belittling my relationship to God by doing this. We don't want our prayers to be those "vain repetitions" Jesus spoke of here. For instance, do you have any phrases you use in prayer that are just habitual and no longer resonate with meaning? In my teen years, I started every prayer with "Father, thank You for this day." It was a word habit, not something that I actually meant in my heart each time I prayed. It seems a little ironic to me that this very chapter has the Lord's Prayer. I think many of us have quoted, "Our Father, who art in heaven, hallowed be thy name . . ." with thoughtless repetition. Remembering the meaning of words we speak in prayer assures our soul connects to the dialogue with God. So understand that these ideas are not your formula but practices that can strengthen your prayer experience.

Examples of how we can pray scripture permeate today's lesson. My heart feels vulnerable right now, because it feels like I am allowing you to invade my private prayer closet. I think this particular day truly represents me the most intimately of any day in this study. I don't begin to think I am the prayer example to follow, but the only way I know to attempt to teach this is to talk about my personal experiences.

Let's say I have an unforgiving heart toward a particular person. I might want to pray Jaron and the Long Road to Love song. Have you heard it? "I pray your brakes go out running down a hill. I pray a flowerpot falls from the window sill, and knocks you in the head like I want to."[5] How I laugh when I hear that song. Haven't we all wanted to pray that for someone?

But my prayers sound more like, "God, You sent Jesus to die for me in the middle of my mess. Jesus told us to forgive seventy times seven. Jesus also told us that we will be forgiven to the degree that we forgive others. I know I can forgive this person by the power of your cross at work inside me, but Lord, my heart is resisting and I am holding on to the anger and wound. Help me to obey Your Word in all these things, love my enemy, forgive them as You forgave me, tossing their wrong as far as the east is from the west." There are six scriptures in that one prayer.

Sometimes I just literally pray a specific passage for someone. Psalm 139 is a favorite: "Julie is not feeling You right now, Lord. Help her to know that You know every hair on her head. Help her to know that You see when she sits down and rises. You discern her heart from afar."

Tragedy might bring a prayer from 2 Corinthians 1:5–6. "Father, may Julie share in Your suffering, so that she can abundantly share in Your comfort."

---

5   Jaron and the Long Road to Love, "Pray for You," sung by Jaron Lowenstein, produced by Big Machine Records through Jaronwood in partnership with Universal Republic, 2009.

If I am struggling with believing I am capable of accomplishing a particular task, my prayer might just be, "Father, You tell me I can do all things through Christ. Help me to live that out today as I teach."

Again, this is not a formula. But for me personally, I don't like asking without recognizing God's power and relationship to the person before asking. So this is my version of *not my will, but thine.* "Father, You know Julie. You know every piece of her. You can change this in an instant. I ask You to . . ." This has never been conscious scripture praying, but this is me saying to God, "I know Your ways are higher than my ways. I know You know every hair on her head much better than I do. I know Your power is way beyond this simple thing I am asking. I know Your plans are to prosper her. I trust You in what You choose to do, but I want You to do (this specific thing)." I am stating my full dependence on Him and faith and confidence in Him before I ask. It is my prayer practice, offering an example of a group of truths I solidly believe: I believe You. My faith is in You. Your will is best. Your power rocks my world! I am going to ask!

There is an intangible experience in my heart when I pray scripture. My heart aligns more readily with God's desires. Notice I did not say aligns perfectly, but I sense genuine transformation inside of me. Later in this study, we spend a week on how prayer changes us. Here, we attempt to practice praying scripture specifically.

Now, it is your turn to practice. If you have a verse you would like to pray, either write it out here, or speak it out loud to God. If you don't like to write, and are in a place you can't speak the prayer, say it in your heart.

If you don't have a verse, pray one or all three, praying to remember who God made you to be. Pray Psalm 139: 13–18.

Praying for Unbelievers

You might want to look up to compare 2 Corinthians 4:3–6 in ESV to see the word comparison with the prayer below. Here is a way to pray 2 Corinthians 4:3–6 for someone who doesn't know God. Fill in the blanks with the person's name.

"God, if Your gospel is veiled to _____, may he or she not be perishing. May the god of this world not be allowed to blind _____, as an unbeliever. Help _____ to see the light of the gospel of the glory of Christ, who is the image of You. God, help me not to proclaim myself but be a servant for Jesus' sake. May You, let light shine out of _____'s darkness. And may You shine in my heart to give the light of the knowledge of Your glory in the face of Jesus Christ."

Praying in Adoration

Pray Psalm 138, or choose any chapter from Psalm 138 through Psalm 150. Sometimes I go through and praise Him in all twelve chapters, skipping 139 because of length!

If you have prayed scripture a lot over the years, journal about it and find ways you could add this to your prayer journey. If you have not prayed scripture, journal about how this practice might help you.

Don't forget our initial conversation regarding fighting the enemy with scripture. How do these things correlate in your heart and mind today?

I will close today with practicing this in a specific spiritual warfare manner. We are going to read Ephesians 6:10–18 in a unique way.

This may be out of your comfort zone, but can I ask you to put on the armor of God as a conversation with Him in your mind. This may feel silly (a little like a child playing imaginary dress up for a battle play), but just practice your awareness of Him as your heart's intent to prepare you for the spiritual battles of the day. I can't tell you how many times, as I am praying, that I physically lift up my fist as if I am holding my shield of faith. Driving to Bible study one day, I caught myself driving with my left hand. My right hand lifted that shield of faith right there in the car as I prayed.

So read through Ephesians 6:10–18 as a prayer.

In The Amplified Bible, Ephesians 6:15–17 says to:

"and having strapped on your feet the gospel of peace in preparation [to face the enemy with firm-footed stability and the readiness produced by the good news]. Above all, lift up the [protective] shield of faith with which you can extinguish all the flaming arrows of the evil one. And take the helmet of salvation, and the sword of the Spirit, which is the Word of God."

Journal your prayer to God.

Week Three, Day Three:
When Two or More Are Gathered, the Power of Praying Together

Father, help me understand the importance of praying with other people. Help me find people who I could comfortably engage in prayer together.

Read Matthew 18:19–20 and Acts 12:5–16.

Where two or more are gathered in agreement, ask anything.

Today, I am so excited to share a testimony from some friends.

A group of girls from my current church decided to deepen their prayer walk. They met together, listening to some sermons online. They studied some things about prayer and decided to commit to pray for something specific that would allow them to see the glory of God for each person. They went around the room, and each decided on a very specific request. You would not believe the miraculous answers God gave them. One woman prayed for her daughter, who refused to talk about Jesus, that they could have a conversation that weekend. It happened. I wish I could go through every single request. Almost every request had a miraculous answer. Praying together can be powerful!

Have you prayed with anyone? Stories like this remind me how important it is for us to pray together. Who do you pray with? Who could you pray with? Could you be the person at your church who begins to gather people to pray together?

Does this intimidate you because you are afraid to pray out loud?

These days there are many options for praying together. A dear friend in New England sent e-mail prayers. It seemed so impersonal to me at first, but now prayers e-mailed and texted from my phone are a part of most days. It is crucial that we spend time with God alone, as Jesus reminded us in Matthew 6, but there is a time to pray together. Journal a prayer about the obstacles that keep you from praying with someone, and pray for ideas of someone you could pray with.

Week Three, Day Four:
We've Got the Power!

Father, help me to know when and how to best exercise the power You give me.

You might think that I mention *Bruce Almighty* too much. Do not be scared. I know it is not a movie that presents great theological truths, but it does make me laugh. In the storyline, God gives Bruce His power, which only covers a few city blocks. Bruce uses this power to turn his car into a Lamborghini, move traffic, split his tomato soup into the two sides of his bowl like the Red Sea, and many other things. And to one man who annoyed Bruce, he did unspeakable things.

Though it might be fun to be empowered that way, how do you experience God empowering you?

Let's look at a specific way God empowered Paul in Acts. Read Acts 13:6–12. How do Paul's words in prayer strike you?

Paul spoke with authority. He recognized the situation, then spoke God's will upon this man. Jesus set an example for this same concept. Read Luke 4:33–35. Jesus commanded the demon to come out. In the other gospels, Jesus tells us to command the mountains to move as well.

Who was involved for Paul to make the authoritative statement in Acts 13:9?

The Holy Spirit empowered Paul's authoritative statement. The Holy Spirit also empowers us. I struggled with adding this page because authoritative prayer is so abused in our culture.

Bruce Almighty abused God's power in the movie. But authoritative prayer abuse in our culture today is perpetrated by those of us who are supposed to know better—believers. The problem with this is that Christianity loses credibility to the nonbelieving world. If we say authoritative healing will come, and it doesn't, we look foolish, confirming what someone might already believe about us. We have made our God look bad, and there is no reason for our God to look bad. Praying this way "assumes" God will do what *our* desire in the situation is, and that does not fit with last week's lesson of "not my will, but thine."

Big caution lights flash in my heart about stating definitively God will or will not do something specific. It is not because I don't have faith God will answer prayer to heal a person, protect someone, or grant a particular blessing. It is because I have faith God knows better than I do in every circumstance. He might heal someone's sickness, but He may intend to use that sickness as He did Paul's thorn in the flesh we studied earlier. God may direct you to pray out loud with authority about a specific thing. Only God sees the whole picture. Sometimes the disciples spoke miraculous healing, and other times they prayed and the person died. Please don't be a person who pretends to perfectly recognize the hand of God. You and I are not better than the disciples. We are to use extraordinary wisdom and discernment. Richard Foster explained it this way: "We must never become so enamored by the spiritual world that we think every jot and tittle of life is caused by supernatural activity, nor should we be so taken in by the naturalistic assumptions of modern society that we fail to see the markings of the transcendent."[6]

We might do this by ascribing every temptation or struggle to Satan. James 1:14 says, "But each person is tempted when he is lured and enticed by his own desire." Sometimes we just desire doing something wrong. Sometimes Satan is coming at us. How do you know the difference?

---

6   Richard Foster, *Prayer: Finding the Heart's True Home* (New York: HarperCollins Publishers, 1982).

With the caveats given, in what ways or things do you see the miraculous power of God in your prayer life?

I must push journaling again, because if you have a record of what you asked, it is much easier to see the answers. Later in the study, we will cover faith in depth. Almost every time Jesus performed a miracle, He said, "according to your faith." The shield of faith did what in Ephesians 6? It "extinguished the flaming darts of the enemy." Believing God to answer your prayer has power. And Jesus said we only had to have faith the size of a mustard seed, right? The ladies I talked about in Day 3 this week laugh about how they really didn't think God was going to answer their requests. But they chose to obey and ask, and guess what? They saw the power of God! I do not think any one of them will ever be the same again.

Do you ever pray with authority like Paul or Jesus did here?

How would you, or do you, discern when or if it is the right time to pray with authority like this?

Can I ask for you to pray boldly here, trusting in the power of God? What is something you really want that only God can do?

Remember James 4:3: "You ask and do not receive, because you ask wrongly, to spend it on your passions." Now that we've reviewed that verse, look up Jesus' words in John 14:13–14. Having read Jesus' words, ask God for something, boldly and believing.

Week Four: Meditation

Teaching Session Four: Living Meditation

1. Worldly meditation focuses on _____ and _____.
   Biblical meditation focuses on _____.

2. Today's Hebrew word for meditate: _____

3. Meditate means to _____, ponder, _____
   _____, imagine, _____, mutter, analyze,
   or _____.

4. Objects of Meditation
   _____/_____ of God

   Joshua 1:8

   Psalm 1:2

   _____ of God

   Psalm 63:6

   _____ of God

   Psalm 77:12

   Psalm 143:5

5. Obstacles of Meditation
   Lack of _____

   Lack of _____

   Lack of _____

If your belief is in your _____ and _____, .
you will not pray. If your belief is in _____ to be at work
_____ you, you will take the time to pray.

Lack of _____

6. Challenge: Can you pray for an hour?

Memory Verse

"Be still, and know that I am God" (Psalm 46:10a).

Week Four, Day One:
Read

Father, as I read Your Word today, engage my heart.

In Week One, do you remember Jesus repeatedly retreating from the crowd? You and I retreat from the crowd this week to quiet our soul and focus our minds and hearts upward. This time we are not studying meditation, but *practicing*.

Remember to focus your heart on one or more of the three objects:

Law/Word of God
Person of God
Works of God

If you attended the teaching session this week, you heard the story about my perceptions of the word *meditation*. You can skip the next paragraph as I retell that story for anyone who missed the teaching session.

Some of you may be like I was at one time. Apprehension arises when the word *meditate* comes up in Christian circles. When we were moving from Texas to Massachusetts, an online search led me to a particular church. A prayer team led by a certain lady was listed. In an e-mail response to my initial inquiry, she mentioned meditation sessions. Even though I certainly knew meditation was a biblical principle and even practiced it, I must confess there was tremendous trepidation in my heart. Images of women sitting in yoga clothes, bending their bodies in a way that mine will not bend, and focusing on their "inner selves" to achieve oneness with the spotted owl and the trees in their yard filled my head. I could not have been more wrong, and that "certain lady" became a dear friend. That church also became home during our time in New England.

My request is that you will not follow my example. Please do not allow the word *meditation* to prevent you from practicing something that can be a life-changing discipline. If you had any hesitation, hopefully you are working through it. Meditation. "Be still, and know that I am God" (Psalm 46:10). Practicing quiet. What do these words elicit in you? Review the obstacles from the teaching session: lack of practice, lack of priority/margin, lack of belief in what He can do, lack of sleep.

Which ones are obstructing the quieting of your heart?

Could you give me a little tolerance through these next few days of homework? This homework poses its own unique challenge. Meditating on the Word of God is an age-old Christian practice, but one many of us have not learned. Whether you are a couch potato or a task-oriented overachiever or anywhere in the middle, consider this week to be a training course in biblical meditation. Please allow me to be your spiritual trainer to increase your meditation muscle. Physical exercise trains our bodies to work better. As believers, meditation means we are relinquishing sin and training ourselves to align our hearts and minds with God.

Most of us are not fans of our trainers through the training process. Please bear with me. When you feel like you cannot be quiet for one more minute, hold on. You can do it! If you fall asleep, start again. Do not give up!

Your four training sessions this week will be on only one passage of scripture as follows:

Day One: Read
Day Two: Reflect
Day Three: Respond
Day Four: Rest

Isaiah 30:15–18 is a passage I suggest because it pertains to the very concept of resting. But if you want to choose your own passage, it can be just about anything—one verse or a long story. It could be a Psalm. One friend did Philippians 4. My only suggestion would be to refrain from any passage that has had great significance to you in the past. As we train, we are attempting to work muscles that have not had much exercise. A not-so-familiar passage helps you hear the Word afresh.

Write your passage here, either the version of Isaiah you prefer or your own chosen passage.

Pray that the concepts you personally need would settle in your heart and mind this week. Do not be the person who just reads these words—actually pray!

Read your chosen passage out loud *slowly* as a conversation with God.

After reading it out loud, read it at least four more times very slowly, including God as you read.

As we strengthen our meditation muscles here, continue reading the passage over and over in prayer for whatever time you are able. Do not hesitate to read different versions for fresh perspectives.

Week Four, Day Two:
Reflect

Father, Holy Spirit, make me aware of what should touch my heart in this passage.

C. S. Lewis wrote: "We live, in fact, in a world starved for solitude, silence, and private: and therefore starved for meditation and true friendship."[7]

I am not naturally a patient person. My impatience parades itself most improperly when I am forced to listen to information I already know. Why my reaction to weeding through known information is so poor is unknown to me. If you have similar issues, read and take in this definition of reflection as we repeat our reading. Today's entire homework is to reread *slowly and intentionally* and to reflect on the passage in prayer. Let's review a few definitions of reflection from the Bing Dictionary.

Reflection
[ri-**flek**-sh*u*h n][8]

noun
1.   the act of reflecting, as in casting back a light or heat, mirroring, or giving back or showing an image; the state of being reflected in this way.
2.   an image; representation; counterpart.
3.   a fixing of the thoughts on something; careful consideration.
4.   a thought occurring in consideration or meditation.

---

7   C. S. Lewis, *The Weight of Glory* (New York: HarperCollins Publishers, 1976).
8   Dictionary.com, "reflection," http://dictionary.reference.com/browse/reflection

Reflection is our goal today. As you digest this definition, slowly and prayerfully reread and reflect on the passage of scripture from yesterday.

Journal your thoughts and reflections on this passage. Tomorrow, we will work on response. No answers needed today, just simple thinking about whatever surfaces in your heart.

Week Four, Day Three:
Respond

Father, what should my response be to this scripture?

Responding. We have spent two days on these words of scripture. So far, you have read and reflected; now is time for the response. Do you have a response to this scripture? Is there something you need to learn?

Reread the passage with thoughts in mind of what your response should be. Don't pressure yourself into a forced response. Is your mind still contemplating? Response can show up in change of heart or change of behavior.

How does your life come in alignment with this passage?

Spend time in prayer working through the response. Pray or journal, whichever will be the most meaningful for you today.

Week Four, Day Four:

Rest

Father, quiet my mind to rest in the truth You have shown me.

"Be still, and know that I am God" (Psalm 46:10). We are putting feet to this scripture today. No runner's feet, as we are being still, but training session four begins now. Let's make those miniscule meditation muscles massive! No steroids required.

Tips for the restless:

- I prefer music without words when I am attempting to relax in scripture, but do not hesitate to try your favorite music. Remember quiet is the goal, so rock music might not be your first choice.

- Remember the rules: NO GUILT ALLOWED! If you need a scripture reminder: "There is therefore now no condemnation for those who are in Christ Jesus. For the law of the Spirit of life has set you free in Christ Jesus from the law of sin and death" (Romans 8:1–2).

- Take time to breathe in and breathe out as you begin. Relax the muscles where you carry tension.

- If you are going to worry about time or your schedule, set a timer.

- Having a pen and paper to write helps me maintain focus. Even if I only write a word or two, my thoughts wander less. Sometimes the writing is doodling.

You may have had little response yesterday, and that's okay. So, you may be trying to figure out how to rest in it. What does that mean exactly? What do you do? Here is a suggestion. Chuck Swindoll, a well-known Christian author stated, "In place of our exhaustion and spiritual fatigue, God will give us rest. All He asks is that we come to Him . . . that we spend a while thinking about Him, meditating on Him, talking to Him, listening in silence, occupying ourselves with Him—totally and thoroughly lost in the hiding place of His presence."[9]

Reread the scripture one more time. Do whatever helps you quiet your mind and relax knowing the truth. Journal. Relax. Review. Reflect. Be still and know the truths God has shown you this week. Rest in those truths. If this seems unlikely for you, set a timer!

After you complete your resting in scripture, there is a Nerd Alert on the next page pertaining to what you have done this week.

On your mark, get set, go! Journal here if you would like.

I hope you are sensing the peace that coincides with knowing He is God. You have completed four training sessions. Congratulations!

Nerd Alert

Surprise! What you have practiced this week is a spiritual tradition among monks since the third century AD. *Lectio Divina* is a Latin term meaning "divine reading." Please do not be distracted by these words or that it was practiced by monks. Understand that Christian monks were professional "pray-ers" or servers of others. Though foreign to us in our culture, the monastic tradition practiced many things that we busy believers in the twenty-first century can use. It is simply a practice of reading, reflecting, responding, and resting in scripture.

Let's remember that worldly meditation focuses on inner self or nature. We are focusing on the Greek word *hawgaw*, from the teaching session that taught us to focus on the truth of God, person of God, and acts of God.

Read, reflect, respond, and rest. *Lectio Divina.* Divine reading.

---

9   Fggam.org, Inspiration, The Quote of the Day, "Chuck Swindoll," http://www.fggam.org/2015/03/the-quote-of-the-day-in-place-of-exhaustion-and-spiritual-fatigue-god-will/

Week Five:
Fasting

Teaching Session Five: Uh Oh, Not the S Word!

1. _____ thinking when ignoring the truth is nothing more than _____.

2. Be honest with yourself about your _____.

3. Denial of _____ is a denial of _____.

   • 1 John 1:8–10

   • When we deny sin, not only are we missing out on _____ and _____, but we forget our need for _____ with _____.

   • 2 Kings 22–23, Josiah loses the law.

4. Not only have we forgotten what is _____ and _____, we have forgotten there is _____ and _____.

   Scriptural examples: Jesus, James 4:2–4, Colossians 3, Revelation churches

5. Acknowledging sin does not mean you are _____ by _____. Jesus defined you!

6. The law was given to _____.

7. Nonbelievers do not need our _____. They need our _____.

8. Show them _____ by being _____ about your sin, and living out God's _____ as an act of _____.
   1 Peter 2:9–10

Memory Verse

"'Yet even now,' declares the Lord, 'return to me with all your heart, with fasting, with weeping, and with mourning'" (Joel 2:12).

Write out this verse in the translation of your choice:

In the last two weeks, we have covered how we can emulate Jesus by prayer and meditation. This week, we will cover the next two items from the list on Week One, Day Two: preparing yourself for temptation by prayer and fasting, and consulting God prior to big decisions.

Week Five, Day One:

Resisting Temptation by . . . Fasting?

Father, help me to understand my temptations and how fasting relates.

Temptation and sin, words not referenced often in our culture today, are the topics of discussion. I wish we could sit around my kitchen table over a cup of coffee, or your beverage of choice, and talk about these words. Pop culture today promotes relativism—if it feels good, do it. Whatever is right *to* you is right *for* you. As much as I would love that conversation around my table, particularly in light of what the Bible has to say, that is not the topic for today. For this day, the discussion about temptation and sin is solely to see how we can follow Jesus' prescription for temptation preparation.

If you would like to reread the verses about the forty days in the wilderness and the temptation of Christ, read Luke 4:1–14. Our focus is simply on Jesus' fasting found in verse 2.

The Renovaré Bible (NRSV) defines fasting as abstaining from something that is part of normal function for the purpose of intense spiritual activity or focus.

Abstaining. Abstinence. These are virtually nonexistent these days. Why would we deny our appetites? Whether we overindulge in food, lack of food, alcohol, cleaning, TV, Internet, buying more, exercise, laziness, or anything else, we are a culture of bigger—more is better. What if we reviewed the addictions or "-aholic" terms? Video game addict, drug addict, sex addict, food addict, work-aholic, rage-aholic, shop-aholic. Our overindulgences are not controlled very well. We love our excesses. I confess my sarcasm, but we are overaddicted, right? We are obsessive-compulsive. It is our genetic disposition—who we are. Do you believe you cannot make a different choice?

Jesus exemplifies a totally different system in the first verses of Luke 4. How did he prepare and deal with temptation? He does not eat, and He prays for forty days and nights.

So, let's return to our definition of fasting: abstaining from something that is part of normal function for the purpose of intense spiritual activity or focus. No doubt Jesus spent those forty days and nights focusing on God and scripture. His response to temptation is scripture, but do not miss that He is fasting also.

While vacationing in the mountains of northeastern Arizona, we left electronics at home in order to focus on our family. Let's look at fasting from this perspective. Fasting is not intended to deprive you of something as much as it is intended to allow you to focus that attention on something else. In the same way we chose to refrain from electronics usage so that we would not be distracted from each other, with fasting we choose to free up time to focus on God.

"One way to begin to see how vastly indulgent we usually are is to fast. It is a long day that is not broken by the usual three meals. One finds out what an astonishing amount of time is spent in the planning, purchasing, preparing, eating, and cleaning up of meals."[10]

Unfortunately, my history with fasting has not always been a win. Often, the deprivation demands my attention and the desired focus turns to the very thing I am attempting to resist. I have not done a forty-day fast before. However, I am confident that in Jesus' humanity, He had moments of desiring something to eat. Scripture clearly states He was hungry. He chose a different focus.

In your own attempts, if your thoughts wander, remember that we are practicing discipline again. Do not give up! No guilt is allowed. This is another training session. Yes, there is a little smirk in my heart at us. We clearly understand fasting to be a discipline, don't we? Training and practice are required.

From what could you abstain that might help you focus?

What is a realistic place for you to begin the discipline of fasting?

---

10   ChristianQuotes.com, Quotes about Fasting, "Elisabeth Elliot," http://www.christian-quotes.info/quotes-by-topic/quotes-about-fasting/

Nerd Alert

As early as the second century AD, history records regular fasting and prayer, particularly prior to Easter. At first, some churches practiced forty hours and others forty days. By the fourth century, with Christianity legalized in Rome in AD 313, this tradition was cemented as a forty-day practice and was officially labeled Lent or Lenten.

Scripturally, the significance of forty days did not only come from Jesus' temptation. It rained forty days and nights during the Flood. (Abstinence from land?) Moses fasted and prayed for forty days in Exodus 34:28. Elijah fasted forty days and nights as he walked to the Mount of God in 1 Kings 19:8. Jonah predicted Nineveh's destruction in forty days in Jonah 3:4, but Nineveh's king declared a fast and told his people to turn from their evil ways in chapter 3. The result after forty days? It stopped raining. Moses understood the law. Elijah heard God in a still, small voice. Nineveh was rewarded with not being destroyed. Jesus headed out, "full of the Holy Spirit," prepared for ministry to begin.

Interestingly, forty-year periods mentioned in scripture come in forms of resting or chastisement. The Israelites wandered forty years in the wilderness after they disobeyed God. Three times in the book of Judges, the people were rewarded for turning back to God with forty years of rest. (Judges records the period of Israel's history when they were ruled by judges prior to them being ruled by kings.) The periods of the kings had forty years of punishment and periods of rewarding rest. And there were forty years between Jesus' death and the destruction of Jerusalem.

How fascinating that Jesus prepared for His ministry by fasting and retreating, while being tempted at the same time. Correlating sin, temptation, fasting, and rest, the number forty throughout scripture repeatedly reiterates these concepts.

Today, fasting is practiced in many different ways. The practice of Lent in Catholicism and some Protestant churches is done by fasting from different food choices for forty days before Easter. In Catholic tradition, it often begins with a reading of the temptation of Christ. I did not grow up in a denomination that practices Lent, but have attended some churches that do and some that do not. Whether we do or do not practice Lent, hopefully, these concepts will expand and grow our understanding of fasting.

Week Five, Day Two:
Abstaining from Schedule

Father, does my schedule need any changes?

The text is still Luke 4. Yesterday, we talked about abstaining from food and other things. Today, we are talking about our schedule. Did that prayer cause a little shiver to run up your spine? It did to mine.

When Jesus went out to the wilderness for forty days and forty nights, He was not only abstaining from food, He was abstaining from whatever His daily schedule had been. Have you ever thought about that? The gospel writers do not specify Jesus' process. He was a carpenter. Completing His earthly projects before He began His heavenly project, I do not see our Lord neglecting any responsibilities. Jesus heads out on His three-year mission that would forever change our world. But before this larger-than-life mission, He begins by abstaining from life as He had known it.

Admittedly, Jesus' spiritual assignment certainly loomed large.

Do you currently have any spiritual assignments or responsibilities?

How could praying and fasting help you clarify or empower them?

If Jesus needed fasting concerning temptation, what are the reasons you do not need to practice fasting and retreating?

I wonder how much clarity Jesus had before His forty-day abstinence from life as He had known it. What did He know of the plan? I wonder which information for His mission came from these forty days. The Bible does not clarify when He knew the specifics, but it does clarify that He spent a tremendous amount of time with His heavenly Father. From my own experiences with God, I believe His clarity for direction came from those times.

We know Jesus abstained from His schedule for these forty days and forty nights. He retreated. What would truly retreating from your schedule require?

Are arguments dancing in your head preemptively in fear that I might ask you to abstain from your schedule? They are in mine: my son's football game, guitar practice, homework, my daughter's flute lessons, play next week, reports due, my own responsibilities from speaking engagements to cleaning the stuff growing in my toilet. *My handsome hubby, Bill, has so much travel, Lord. When could I possibly abstain from my schedule?* Let's not hyperventilate yet; no paper bags required. My schedule is certainly not evil, but looking at Jesus' example of checking out of His schedule to fast and pray before His ministry would begin causes me to take pause. Seeing His regular practice of retreating causes me to scratch my head at the lack of this discipline.

Here is the question: is there a smaller, more realistic way you could incorporate this practice of abstinence, whether a beginner or an experienced retreater?

To be people who abstain from the distractions of our lives, we must plan and be intentional. Particularly if you are in the "mothering" season of life, opportunities do not often present themselves to retreat in this way. Does it strike you as funny that we are discussing being intentional, yet scheduling even as we talk about the lack of a schedule? Paradoxes permeate scripture. Grace versus diligence, generosity versus responsibility, and being intentional with no schedule. It may be a counter-intellectual endeavor, but it is not counter to God's repeated recommendation to pray and include Him. We are reviewing so many of those scriptures in this study that I will spare you the list here.

Friends, family, and advisors' opinions might differ about how we should prioritize our schedules. In 2001, just after the Twin Towers had come down, my daughter was six weeks old and my son was two and a half. As we transitioned from Memphis, Tennessee, to Dallas, Texas, my husband was working in Dallas, while I stayed in Memphis to sell the house. You can imagine my state of mind with a newborn and a two-year-old after being hospitalized for a week with postpartum eclampsia. This hypertension induced from pregnancy is the most common way women die from childbirth, so it certainly couldn't be ignored.

Five weeks later, while showing the house, managing two small children, being emotional after 9/11, and my husband out of town, shooting chest pain struck. My doctor had been very direct about how quickly to respond to chest pain. After scampering for child care, my dad escorted me to the ER. My blood pressure was dramatically elevated, though thankfully not enough to be hospitalized again. The doctor instructed, "You are stressed. You need to take a walk by yourself for an hour every morning, and you need to make sure you get enough sleep." If your mouth is not agape right now, you might reread my circumstances. A doctor, with years of education, believed it was realistic for me, the mother of an infant and a two-year-old, to go on a walk *by myself* in the morning and to get enough sleep. Did he think I could twitch my nose for my husband to appear from out of town? Did he think two year olds and infants could take care of themselves? Did he think sleep deprivation was something new mothers opted to have? Did he think moving across the country and selling our house while a war began from a national catastrophe might not be stressful? I was amazed I did not have a heart attack right there!

Please consider and recognize your point in life. You have earthly responsibilities, and those are God-given. Find ways to prioritize retreating and fasting in your life. But do not neglect your children, family, or other responsibilities. Evaluate which responsibilities need to be prioritized and which ones need to vaporized.

What are the blocks of time that could be used for fasting or abstinence?

What are the responsibilities or scheduled items you might need to change?

Again, this is not for the purpose of guilt but for us to learn how to prioritize what matters. Look at the following exercise. See if there is something you could do.

Is there any way you could schedule one of these exercises right now? Here are some ideas to start:

- Fast from sugar or a specified item you love for a specified period of time.

- Fast from a single meal or for a few hours.

- Fast for a twenty-four-hour period when your schedule is not as demanding. (My choice is usually 5p.m.–5p.m.)

- Choose an early morning or late night window of time when you could commit to journaling your heart in words and prayer to God.

- Pick a passage of scripture to meditate on while retreating for thirty minutes.

- Fast from television or computers or both for a certain period of time.

- Fast from that TV show you knew you shouldn't have been watching anyway.

- Fast from the radio in the car and focus on prayer time.

When you schedule this exercise, try to come back and note anything about it that stood out.

Week Five, Day Three:

The Bridegroom Is Away

Father, open my heart to the meaning of your physical absence and the presence of Your Holy Spirit.

My pastor in New England, Chris Mitchell, often spoke of a story. Frightened in the middle of the night, a little girl called out for her parents. As Mom lovingly comforted her precious daughter, she reminded her that God is always with her. Scared and unsure, the daughter responded, "Mommy, I know God is with me, but I wanted someone with skin."

Have you felt this way? My heart pleads for signs and wonders to demonstrate God's skin to me. I want to feel those huge arms of God wrapped around me. The disciples had that privilege—God's skin, Jesus in the flesh. As our discussion centers on fasting and the bridegroom's exit, let's review some passages.

> And they said to him, "The disciples of John fast often and offer prayers, and so do the disciples of the Pharisees, but yours eat and drink." And Jesus said to them, "Can you make wedding guests fast while the bridegroom is with them? The days will come when the bridegroom is taken away from them, and then they will fast in those days." (Luke 5:33–35)

C. S. Lewis, a well-known Christian intellectual and writer, said, "This Man (Jesus) suddenly remarks one day, 'No one need fast while I am here.' Who is this Man who remarks that His mere presence suspends all normal rules?"[11] Do you

---

11   Christasus.com, What Are We to Make of Jesus Christ?, from "God in the Dock" by C. S. Lewis, http://www.christasus.com/letters/cslwhatarewetomakeofjesuschrist.htm

believe that His presence suspended all rules? His presence *does* suspend all rules! Does it not? Do you believe that?

Jesus said to Thomas, "Have you believed because you have seen me? Blessed are those who have not seen and yet have believed" (John 20:29).

You and I fit in both of these categories if we are believers. Our Bridegroom is no longer present, and we believe. With the absence of His physical presence, I eagerly yearn for the skin of my Jesus. Though it does not refer to fasting, read Romans 8:18–28 concerning this yearning and the work of the Holy Spirit. As we will be spending an entire week on the Holy Spirit later, I don't want to dwell on it here. Just be reminded that our closest experience of God's skin is His Spirit.

How and why does fasting fit into our longing for Jesus' presence and our need for His Spirit?

To get a clearer answer to that question, reread the second paragraph of the Nerd Alert between Day One and Day Two.

What were the results of fasting and prayer for these men?

Jesus:

Moses:

Elijah:

Nineveh:

Fasting, prayer, Jesus' physical absence, God's skin, and Spirit.

Take this time to quiet your mind and think through these items. Anything stand out? Allow your mind and heart to engage with God.

If you are like me, and do not deal well with abstract thinking, please bear with this more artsy, abstract approach. To the artist, take full liberty to make these words into something beautiful.

Write words and draw lines about how these things intersect in your life.

Jesus' Absence

Prayer

Holy Spirit

God's Skin

Fasting

Week Five, Day Four:
Consulting God for Decisions, Particularly Big Ones

Father, give me the wisdom to consult You as I make decisions.

Jesus fasted and prayed for forty days and then began His ministry (Luke 4).

Esther asked the people to fast before she approached the king to defend her people (Esther 4:16).

Nehemiah fasted and prayed before he asked the king to allow him to return to Jerusalem to rebuild the wall (Nehemiah 1).

So many different examples. What are your big decisions these days? Do you retreat to pray or fast over them? Remember rules 1, 2, and 3: No guilt allowed! Do we not beg God for a sign, an open door, or a closed door in our thirty-second prayers? But are we willing to devote ourselves to prayer when God doesn't answer with an immediate yes?

What are your big decisions? Whether it is a move around the world or across the street, a job change or a life change, a life/death decision or a petty one, sincerely fasting and discussing it with God enhances, not distracts from, the process.

What kind of decision maker are you? Are you a business-savvy-go-getter who is decisive and quick? Are you the one who overanalyzes and belabors until the options have changed? Or somewhere in the middle?

Whatever speed or style, your process can either include God or not. Jesus exemplified retreating for forty days before He chose His disciples and began His life change toward ministry. Most of us are not ready for a forty-day fast or a retreat to pray, though I would recommend fasting and retreating. But what can you do? What is a realistic starting point? When can you include this in your schedule?

What decisions or life changes are happening for you?

Are you including God? If so, how? If not, why not?

We read this at the beginning of the study, but remember the persistent widow in Luke 18:1–8. How do you persist in prayer?

We discussed examples from Esther, Nehemiah, and Jesus' life. Take some time to consult God regarding questions in your life. They could be regarding your job, parenting, future, gifting, finances, mission, or anything else. Write some notes below.

Pray now. Speak it or journal it here.

Week Six: Intercession

Teaching Session Six: Praying for Others

1. Petition is praying for _____.

2. Intercession is praying on _____ of _____.

3. Paul says repeatedly, "I am _____."

4. Intercession is the space where _____ and _____ meet.

5. Esteem _____ as better than _____.
   Philippians 2:3

6. Care more about _____ on this earth
   than you care about _____.
   • James 4:3–4
   • Psalm 37:4
   • Revelation 12:11

7. Paul challenged us to pray for _____.

8. _____ is praying for you!

Before you focus on the memory verse this week, please read this in its context, at least the first three verses of Galatians 6. It is a great follow up to Week Four, Day Two, Nerd Alert.

Memory Verse

"Bear one another's burdens, and so fulfill the law of Christ" (Galatians 6:2).

Write out this verse in the translation of your choice:

Week Six, Day One:

Jesus' Last Prayer

*Father, demonstrate today how to love the people around me in a way that I
invest time in sincere prayer for them.*

So far, we have covered Jesus' regular practice of prayer, meditation, fasting, and consulting God in our decision making. Today, we move to intercession—simply the practice of praying for people outside of ourselves. For our scripture texts, we will join Jesus as He dreads going to the cross and talks to His Father about it.

Have you been in a situation when you actually knew something bad was about to happen?

My dear friend's husband was diagnosed with terminal cancer. Our precious friend Bill—lighthearted, life of the party, always the jokester—had metastatic stage four cancer. I can still envision that multicolored clown wig, eighteen inches tall, crowning his short Irish frame every Halloween.

Just days before finding out, we were sledding down a large hill, laughing heartily, both families, kids and adults. We slid backward, forward, attached to each other, holding on and letting go. Pain bothered Bill during those hours, which would soon be diagnosed.

Sadly, my dear friend and her lighthearted husband found themselves waking up in those last days to the anxiety of navigating new symptoms, incapacities, and the emotional roller coaster. Living in the unknown moments awaiting the end challenged them. Praying brought more questions. We did not know how or what to pray. We prayed desperately for the miracle, but wondered if the miracle rescue would be his entrance to heaven. It was. The last day did come.

You and I are heading to the garden to join Jesus in that same place of dread—The Garden of Gethsemane. Jesus was deep in prayer. He knew the hour had come. This prayer was His last words before His arrest, which led to His death. Luke tells us this prayer was accompanied by tears of blood. His account gives us more events than specifics about the prayer. Read Luke 22:39–46 to follow along.

John gives us more detailed words of the prayer. Jesus begged the disciples to stick with Him in prayer. He clearly knew what was coming. He was not looking forward to the horrific hours leading to the cross. Yet, His love for the disciples consumed the words He uttered to His Father. He had great concern for them.

I want you to be right there. Picture it with me, two thousand years ago. Let's *feel* this moment. Please hear Jesus' desperate heart of compassion as He prays for these men whom He *knows* He is about to leave. He *knows* how much fear is going to grip them. He *knows* they are not going to understand what is happening. He *knows* they are going to question their very souls if everything they have believed would actually be true over the next fifty-plus hours. He is interceding for them at this very moment. Do you feel His plea?

Intercession, according to *Webster's Dictionary*, is praying on another person's behalf. Let's move over to the next book and read John's account detailing Jesus' actual intercession as He prays on another person's behalf. Remember, John was right there as these events unfolded. He was likely one who had fallen asleep and been reprimanded by Jesus, but that is not the part of the story he recorded. He recorded Jesus' prayer. Remember to hear Jesus' heart. Read John 17 to get the entire picture of Jesus' prayer.

Let's stick with this a little longer to dig deeper into Jesus' heart revealed for His disciples. Reread John 17: 6–19 and highlight or underline all the times Jesus reminds God about His disciples.

> I have manifested your name to the people whom you gave me out of the world. Yours they were, and you gave them to me, and they have kept your word. Now they know that everything that you have given me is from you. For I have given them the words that you gave me, and they have received them and have come to know in truth that I came from you; and they have believed that you sent me. I am praying for them. I am not praying for the world but for those whom you have given me, for they are yours. All mine are yours, and yours are mine, and I am glorified in them. And I am no longer in the world, but they are in the world, and I am coming to you. Holy Father, keep them in your name, which you have given me, that they may be one, even as we are one. While I was with them, I kept them in your name, which you have given me. I have guarded them, and not one of them has been lost except the son of destruction, that the Scripture might be fulfilled. But now I am coming to you, and these things I speak in the world, that they may have my joy fulfilled

in themselves. I have given them your word, and the world has hated them because they are not of the world, just as I am not of the world. I do not ask that you take them out of the world, but that you keep them from the evil one. They are not of the world, just as I am not of the world. Sanctify them in the truth; your word is truth. As you sent me into the world, so I have sent them into the world. And for their sake I consecrate myself, that they also may be sanctified in truth. (John 17:6–19)

How many phrases did you mark?

Why do you think Jesus reviews these things with the Father?

Jesus' authentic humanity displays itself. My translation of these words goes like this: "Oh, Father, I love these guys. I am leaving them. They may act crazy the next few days, but don't forget who they are. Don't forget who they believe. Don't forget that I have prepared them. I am sending them out. Please protect them."

Do you think Jesus thought the Father was going to forget? I don't think for a second that is the case, but His heart is still calling out for His Dad to remember. Jesus recognizes the necessity of asking, and He demonstrated His passion with tears of blood for more than just Himself.

Recognizing this as an unusual moment of agony for our Savior, I want us to evaluate our own prayer passion for our loved ones.

How does your prayer life for your loved ones look like Jesus'?

How can you improve your prayer for the people you care about?

Take some time here to offer up some heartfelt prayer for people who you consider to be your close relationships, whether family or friends. Before you start, write the names out on paper. I suggest writing these names in your prayer, but do what works the best for you. If there is a physical position that helps you focus, use that posture to help maintain your focus.

I have to tell you, the Nerd Alert on the next two pages rocked my world. I am so thankful I did not miss it. Whether you read it today or tomorrow, I hope you don't miss it either.

Nerd Alert

Kidron Valley/Garden of Gethsemane/Mount of Olives

In this study, we covered the last words of Jesus before His arrest from two different gospels. The location of this prayer offers a significant parallel from Old Testament events to New Testament. When it comes to scripture, seeing how events parallel each other elicits a realization of God's hand in the specifics. In this particular case, they are a thousand years apart. If the thought of geography annoys or challenges you, you can skip this, but I think it might interest you.

John mentions the crossing of the Kidron Valley and the Garden. Luke mentions the Mount of Olives. Look at the picture taken on the Temple Mount looking over the Kidron Valley, facing the Garden of Gethsemane, which is located on the Mount of Olives. The garden is just to the left of the large building in the center of the picture. I wanted to give you a perspective on the closeness of these places. The characters were not covering some great amount of land. The distance is approximately one thousand feet from the temple through the valley up to the garden. For the math-challenged, that is just a little more than three football fields attached, or one-fifth of one mile.

Many things of biblical significance occurred in this region. During Passover, which was being celebrated the weekend of Jesus' arrest, all the sacrifices would surround the temple. The blood of the animals would literally run down into the Brook Kidron in the valley Jesus was crossing. In the Old Testament, idols had been burned repeatedly here, leaving dust in the Brook

Kidron. The Kidron Valley represented sin and sacrifice. In 2 Samuel 15, King David and his people fled from his son, Absalom, who was attempting to steal the throne. David and his supporters grieved, leaving Jerusalem as they crossed the Kidron and headed up the Mount of Olives. The people had brought the Ark of God with them, but David insisted it be returned to the temple. David trusted in God's plan, whether it meant David's throne was returned or not. David wept and prayed. God responded and restored David's kingdom.

We don't know if it was this exact spot, but Jesus also wept and prayed as He crossed over the Kidron, per the hand of John. He was about to restore the kingdom by being the blood sacrifice during Passover weekend. Though David's kingdom restoration was to a physical throne, Jesus' kingdom restoration brought all of humankind forever to God, the True King.

In the Kidron Valley, the prayers of David and Jesus parallel one another. The kingdom restoration parallels. And the two stories are bridged by thousands of years of blood sacrifices until Jesus, once and for all, through His blood sacrifice, breaks the need for sacrifices.

Week Six, Day Two:

Jesus' Prayer for Peter

Father, teach me how to pray for the people I love.

Yesterday, we saw an overview of Jesus' last prayer and focused specifically on His heart and words for His disciples. I hope you also read the Nerd Alert about the amazing connection of Old to New Testament in the Kidron Valley. Today, we are going to look at a specific prayer for one of those disciples—Peter. We begin with Peter's denial of Christ. If you want to see or revisit the specifics, read Luke 22:54–62).

Oh, the look of Jesus. How I do not want to look at the face of my Savior while the stench of sin is fresh on my breath! Just hours earlier, Peter heard Jesus' groaning and heartfelt prayer. He had witnessed His stress-induced sweating of blood. And Peter finds himself. Here. Guilty. Broken.

What have you experienced with God that would compare to where Peter finds himself?

How did you respond?

Forgive me that we are backtracking today. I hope this is one of those times that knowing the future brings clarity to the past. We are reading about the Last Supper, which happened before the garden scene that we read yesterday. In the garden, Jesus prayed for His disciples, but at this meal, He addressed Peter specifically before the denial. Read Luke 22:31–34 about the disciples squabbling, yet again, about who is the best among them.

Did you notice how Jesus did not pray for Peter to *not* deny? Jesus did not pray for Peter to correct his behavior. Jesus did not pray for Satan to not sift him. Jesus did not even condemn Peter's denial.

What are three things Jesus said to Peter in verse 32?

Did you catch all three phrases?

1. His faith would not fail
2. When he had turned back (repented)
3. Strengthen his brothers

Do you sense the reprieve Jesus allowed for Peter to gather himself in the middle? He did not direct or pray for his immediate turning back. He said "when you have turned back," giving Peter the reprieve to turn back in his own time. Jesus verbalized unwavering confidence that Peter would repent. How do you give yourself time and space to "turn back"?

How do you currently use prayer to recuperate from the moments you want to turn away?

If these answers are all similar for you, do not be concerned. How do you respond differently in prayer in moments of egregious failure?

We have used these words to be introspective about our own prayer life. How can we use these concepts as we pray for others?

Write the names of two to five people you would consider to be in your inner circle.

Peter was in Jesus' inner circle here on earth. Review the three things Jesus said again. How can you use Jesus' example in the way you pray for your inner circle?

Take time to write out a prayer or pray diligently for these individuals.

Week Six, Day Three:
Having Spiritual Eyes

Father, help me to grasp Your work in the world and my role in the furtherance of Your kingdom.

So far this week, we have looked at Jesus' words to God in the garden and to Peter during the Last Supper. Remember His passionate heart for His disciples. Today, we are rewinding the clock a little further to review Jesus' command to pray for another group of people.

The context is long for this passage, but if you want to read the whole story, read Luke chapters 9 and 10. If you just want to cover the material for today, read Luke 10:2.

Who do you think Jesus is referring to when He uses the terms *laborers*, *farmhands*, or *harvest workers*, depending on your translation?

Do you pray for God's provision of workers for His kingdom?

How much time do you genuinely pray for God's work to be accomplished?

Many years ago, I walked into a Singles Bible Study Fellowship. Most people were my age (at the time), in their 20s and early 30s. I thought I recognized the guy leading music, but I could not place him. I don't know what happens to you when you *know* you should know someone, but for me, obsessiveness takes over. I couldn't focus on the worship because I was trying to remember how I knew him. The reels of my mind were trying to rewind to whatever spot on the reel he was, but to no avail.

Thankfully, he approached me afterward to say that I had led him to Jesus when we were in high school. It was a very surreal moment. After some discussion, I realized a dear friend had dragged me along on a social visit because these two friends often had faith discussions. I must tell you I do not remember a single thing I said to this person. He did not pray with us that day. But I do remember praying for him many times.

Oddly, my affinity for cars often reminds me to pray for someone. When a car like his passed, I would take the opportunity to pray for him to know Jesus. I did not remember his face. I did not remember the discussion. I did not remember much about him. The prayer was a simple, "Lord, help Him to recognize You." Standing in a church I had never visited, God showed me that He answered the tiniest of prayers through a boy-turned-man whom I did not remember.

This monumental God-moment etched itself forever in my memory. When I went home that night, many names and faces flooded my recollection. My Muslim neighbors, an atheist friend's entire family, and another friend had all come to believe in Jesus. A roommates' family, who were geographically far from us and far from Christ, had one by one come to know our faith. Most miraculously, my good friend's dad accepted Christ right before he was diagnosed with lung cancer and died just months later. These were not people with whom I had shared the Good News, but people for whom I had prayed. The long list overwhelmed me. I sensed the reminder that God was much better at changing people's lives than I would ever be. I might be able to discuss reasons for faith. I might be able to answer questions. I might be able to intellectually argue why God is real. But He could meet every person with or without my participation. Calling on Him accomplished more than anything I had ever spoken or anything I could do! Prayer powered accomplishments that I could not make.

Whether the work God has you doing is feeding the poor, sharing the message of Jesus, rescuing those trapped in human trafficking, teaching scripture, taking care of the sick, caring for infants at church, adopting kids, running the coffee shop, or the everyday drudgery of washing dishes and changing diapers, prayer will multiply the work (hopefully not the dirty diapers). But He can do it better than you can.

Do not neglect your God-given passions or giftedness, but make sure prayer permeates the process. What were James' words? "You do not have, because you do not ask" (James 4:2b). How foolish to miss God's power because we simply did not open our mouths to ask! Proverbs speaks often of fools forgetting God. Thank goodness God will forgive us for not including Him in the very thing He has given us the ability to do or the passion to accomplish. But I don't want Him to have to practice forgiveness, I want to remember Him and see His power demonstrated in my gifting and my passions.

We will discuss spiritual gifts in more detail in the Holy Spirit chapter. What are your spiritual gifts? If you don't know, find a time to gather resources at your church to help you.

I didn't recognize for many years what my spiritual gifts were. It's funny looking back now because I taught others from a very young age. When I hear scripture misquoted or truth being twisted to fit somebody's agenda for a message, my soul screams inside me. For many years, I confessed this to God as self-righteousness, apologizing for my wrong spirit toward the teacher. I was in my thirties before I came to understand that anger actually originated from God's gifting to teach. I obsess over details in teaching, study one word for hours, and can be judgmental about poor preparation. What do you get angry or feel passionate about that could be related to your gifting? Passion can look like anger, so think about that as you answer.

What are some practical ways for you to remember to include God in these things?

Week Six, Day Four:

Interceding Instead of Intruding

Father, help me to intercede before I speak and act.

Many of you will relate to the following words: two teenagers. Yes, I know parenting is a gift from God. Yes, I know they are precious and beautiful creations.

Blah . . . blah . . . blah . . .

Of course, I adore them. I could go into another lengthy monologue of how amazing they are. Clearly, I have been given this responsibility by God. But if there is any area of my life I need to ask God's direction before I act, it is parenting. And yet, in the day-in, day-out challenges, the importance of needing God's participation eludes me, and I am too often caught up in the moment. It's my most important God-given responsibility, and I do not remember to consult God. Whether discipline, discussion, laughter, or separating two kids trying to wrestle it out, motherhood shines a spotlight on the ugliest pieces of me. When I stop to pray, my gut reactions subside and I can react in God's strength, not my own. This is the goal: for prayer to permeate our processes, particularly surrounding the roles we perform in the kingdom.

We said yesterday that prayer permeated Paul's process. If we were to go through Acts, we would see repeated redirection and changing of Paul's plan by the Holy Spirit. Let's look at an example in Acts 16. In the interest of context, Timothy has just joined Paul, Silas, and Luke (the writer of Acts) on their missionary journey.

> And they went through the region of Phrygia and Galatia, having been forbidden by the Holy Spirit to speak the word in Asia. And when they had come up to Mysia, they attempted to go into Bithynia, but the Spirit of Jesus did not allow them. (Acts 16:6–7)

Was Paul clearly called to proclaim the Word?

How does this concept of the Holy Spirit and Spirit of Jesus forbidding the Word to be proclaimed affect you?

What does it teach about the importance of walking in the Spirit, with prayer, in what God intends you to do?

God forbidding me to do the very thing He has called me to do seems incomprehensible. And to state the obvious, God knows what we do not. He is not limited by what we can do. He can use anyone or anything, including the rocks, to speak to them. He can send manna from heaven to feed them. You and I, however, are limited.

You may be arguing with me, quoting these words, "I can do all things through him who strengthens me" (Philippians 4:13). However, understand I am not contradicting scripture saying you cannot do all things through Christ. But in our humanness, we mistake our own intentions, especially when they are scriptural and good, for God's. Our intentions are not God's intentions.

Please do not miss the damage this does. These mistakes have costs believers dearly. Many unbelievers have turned their ears away from God because of loudly spoken, well-intentioned sentiments, spoken in God's name. Our words can end up as spouting, erroneous human faith, or inappropriately timed, inconsiderate outpouring of truth. Being slow to speak, even when it is truthful, is still wise. I could cite many examples, from political ones to those epithets and scriptures we pound at people in times of crisis.

Instead of my examples, I give you Holly McRae. Holly spoke at our church about her daughter, Kate, who has recurrent metastatic brain cancer. Kate was diagnosed at five years old, in 2009. Her statistical chances are 3 percent survival with virtually no chance of any quality of life in that survival. As you can imagine, many people have offered words throughout her four-year heart-breaking road.

Holly spoke of well-intentioned believers who quoted scripture and reminded her that God is in control. They said Kate's struggle has a greater purpose and that God was going to use it for good. To a mother whose child is walking through cancer, these things felt cliché. It is not that she didn't know these things were true, but they rang in her heart as a lack of empathy and a demeaning of the moment's hardship. Would you have walked up to Jesus as He sweated blood in the garden and said, "God has a purpose in everything" or "All things work together for good"? As absurd as that sounds, we often offer our answers to someone else's issue. We think we have their answer. We have the book they need to read. We have the right scripture. We have the comparative circumstance they obviously need to hear, right?

Praying and listening can keep us from perpetrating well-intentioned, but ill-timed, truth. Praying, particularly with an awareness of the Holy Spirit, grants wisdom to not speak. Not having the answer often demonstrates the greater wisdom. Not having the answer elevates the other person by quietly deferring and meeting them without any requirement. Grace exemplified. It elevates God too by allowing Him space to comfort them and move apart from our participation.

I believe that if we would stop offering answers and instead offer genuine prayers and grace, we would see the power of God in miraculous ways. In God's game, humility trumps pride. Our "answers" and "wisdom" can keep someone we love from experiencing or hearing our God's amazing grace.

Of course there are times that God will direct us to speak. But if we do not consult Him, we are not following Him. We are just intruding instead of interceding.

So we revisit: Do you have someone needing help around you right now? Have you talked to God about it? Have you sensed the Holy Spirit's direction? Pray right now for His direction.

The next question may challenge you, and it may not even apply, but consider it sincerely. Who do you offer advice to instead of interceding? Right here and now, pray for anyone who comes to mind.

This next one should probably be an entire lesson in itself, but listen to the Holy Spirit as you ponder. Is there anyone you are talking badly about or with whom you are disagreeing? I am not only talking about in a relationship. It could be a political figure, a Hollywood star, or a minister in your church. Take time to pray for them right now.

Week Seven:
Authenticity

Teaching Session Seven: Revealing Raw Reality

Humility + Honest Confession + Recognizing Your Need for God – People Pleasing

= Authenticity

1. Grace _____ the _____.

2. Necessity of _____
   Samuel 22:27–29; Philippians 2:2–4 (MSG)

3. Four Humility Meter Indicators: _____ and
   _____
   Pay attention to your own _____.
   Inability to genuinely _____ someone else
   Belittling _____
   Humility is not self _____, but genuinely _____.

4. Humility acknowledges _____, but doesn't
   _____ in it. It has a proper _____.
   • Find a _____.
   • Ask a _____ or your _____.

5. Honest _____.
   TO GOD—1 John 1:9,
   Ask Him the _____.

TO EACH OTHER—James 5:16

Being _____ with your _____ few.

6. Recognize your ongoing _____ for God.

7. _____

- If your heart is genuinely seeking to please God, you will have a _____ _____ life.

- If your heart is genuinely seeking to please others, you will have a _____ _____ life.

8. Good behavior should be the _____ of your prayer life.

Memory Verse

"Casting all your anxieties on him, because he cares for you" (1 Peter 5:7).

"Create in me a clean heart, O God, and renew a right spirit within me" (Psalm 51:10).

Write out these verses in the translation of your choice:

Chipping away at our list of how Jesus gave us examples of prayer, now we study crying out to God for a change of circumstance. Webster's defines authenticity as genuineness. Authenticity might not be the obvious word for this week, but when we cry out, are we not at our most genuine? Asking for some leniency this week, our week's topics are enveloped by authenticity. Our topics for the week are crying out to God, confession, pride, people-pleasing, and discerning our hearts. If Jesus did not demonstrate any one of these in practice, His prayer or teaching reviews it. Let's delve into these practices connecting the dots to prayer.

Week Seven, Day One:

Crying Out to God

Father, help me to sincerely release frustration at Your feet.

Jesus prayed in the garden of Gethsemane. He cried out to God. We read that text last week, which focused on John's accounts. Read Luke 22:39–46 if you want to remember specifics. (You can read also Mark 14:32–42 and Matthew 26:36–46 if you want to read the other gospel writers' accounts.)

Do you know how to cry out to God? Jesus cried out for another way with sweat and tears, even to the point of blood. He did not want to go to the cross, and He told His Father about it.

Crying out to God was something that did not come naturally to me. I think some of the difficulty came from my mother's well-intentioned words. Her statements rang in my ears: "You better be thankful for how much God has given you" or "No whining," and the absolute intolerance of any complaints. The "American guilt" syndrome landed on so many of us. I also have a younger brother who had severe brain damage from birth, and I carried guilt if I ever complained. That did not come from my parents, but what in the world did I have to complain about? My brother could not walk, talk, or even feed himself.

We do not need to get into the good and bad of that type of thinking, but for me to "cry out to God" about circumstances or a difficult road seemed ludicrous. But belittling the difficulties of my own life meant I began a pattern of pretending everything was good, stuffing heartbreaks and disappointments. I did not learn to release these things to a God who could have certainly helped me more appropriately navigate the challenges of life.

What about you? Many people come out of the womb with a natural bent toward crying out to God, and this can be a very good thing. If you are one of those who releases everything on those around you and God, you might have to watch for what can become a festival of self. Do people around you cringe with hesitation when something goes awry? Though that conversation is for another day, know your own heart as we cover today's material.

Do you tend toward releasing your frustration too readily or quietly keeping it all inside? I can land on either, especially among those closest to me, but God continues to teach me to release those frustrations honestly to Him. (The Bible also says to be truthful with the one who offended or angered you, but that is another lesson too.)

Psalm 88 is the Psalm that has no closure. Read it now.

There is no resolution. The sadness continues. I believe it was left in our amazing book of Psalms for a reason. At times there is not a resolution, and grieving continues for a long time—whether it is a death, a loss, an ongoing challenge, or a combination. Sometimes our situation does not change, and we have to figure out how to navigate the ongoing pain in our souls.

My sister-in-law lost her mother twenty-two years ago, and yet she still misses her and grieves when circumstances strike her memory. Parenting alone after losing a spouse could elicit that long-time challenge. My brother's brain damage was not going to repair itself, and the daily challenges of caring for a long-term patient was difficult for my parents.

We must cry out to our God who hears and understands. Believe that He hears and sees you. *El Roi* is a Hebrew term meaning "the god who sees." This term was first used in the Old Testament when Sarah's maidservant, Hagar, had run away from Abraham and Sarah in Genesis 16:13. God sent an angel to speak to her, and he sent her back to them with a promise that she would bear a son. Hagar cried out to God.

Jesus instructed us about this in Matthew 11:28–30. Read that passage now.

Do you struggle with crying out to God or believing that He hears and sees you? If so, journal or talk to Him here.

Week Seven, Day Two:
Confession Needed: The Pharisee and The Hidden

Father, remind me to confess honestly and learn transparency, particularly when I pray in public.

Please forgive how quick I am throwing us into the scripture today, but there is much to cover, so on your mark, get set, go!

Read Luke 18:9–14.

Before you are too hard on this Pharisee guy, what do you do better than others that you might use to elevate yourself a bit above the people around you? I believe the older we get and the further we get in this journey, the easier it is to think we have it all figured out. Recognizing our need for our God can be difficult.

Years ago, one of my dearest friends, who happens to be nine years younger, had just moved across Texas. Let me make clear that this is someone whom I treasure. Knowing the moving journey well and knowing my extra years of life, I gave no credence to her frustrations and sadness. As she began the very normal loneliness and sadness after a move, I was not mean to her, but I was dismissive in my heart to her struggle.

Why did I react that way? Why did I dismiss someone I love dearly while in the midst of a hard time I should understand well? The arrogant Pharisee burned in my thoughts, *Oh God, help this friend. You already taught me this lesson. I moved much further, and I did not have a single friend within a thousand miles. She has family within a few hours, a dear friend, and her culture still with her. I am older and smarter than she is. Thank You that I am not as pathetic as she is anymore* . . . Of course I did not pray this prayer, but my heart was every bit that ugly.

I had to get down on my face for this one. "God, how could I possibly treat my dear friend so callously when I know how hard it is to move? How could I dismiss her sadness? I confess that arrogant, nasty heart, and thank You for covering my ugliness in spite of me! Help me to be the friend that she needs, not in any way demeaning her or belittling her. Help me to raise her up, recognize her amazing value, and encourage her. Help me to grieve with her for her loss and her sadness. Forgive me for my awful pride."

I confessed, let it go, and let God guide me through restoring my empathy. Thankfully for my friendship, He did!

On the other hand, we are allowed to recognize and acknowledge the realities of where God has matured us, as long as we credit the One who did the work. When we start crediting ourselves or forgetting we still require grace each day, the dangerous, devouring pride creeps into our hearts.

Shed light in those heart places where you have elevated yourself and genuinely begun to rely on your giftedness, maturity, or wisdom. Who is it for you? Who do you believe you are "above"? Your husband, your friends, those younger or older, a political group, someone you see on the street or at church, someone who has not learned a lesson that you already know, someone still caught up in a mire of sin you never participated in, or even your children? It can be just about anyone.

Be honest enough to admit and confess to God who this is in your life. If you have the courage, write the name, group, or wrongdoers here.

If you can muster the humility, pray for the wrongdoer(s).

Every bit as difficult and every bit as pride related, we address next our secret. Shh! What is that secret? Do you have a secret shame or ongoing practice you do not want anyone to know? I must be the bearer of bad news, though I am sure it is bad news you already know. It is not a secret. It is not hidden. God sees. God knows. You may be hiding it from your friends, family, or your church, but you are not hiding it from God. Is it keeping you from talking to Him because you are hesitant to approach our perfect God? Do you think He does not want to talk to you because of it? Confess it. Remember that what He did on the cross is bigger than your secret.

God pulled out His Ace of Spades and trumped everything else by being nailed to a cross. Holding on and hiding implies you believe what you do matters more than what He did, and that is the other side of pride! "I am so bad that my stuff is bigger and worse than anything God could do." Do you see the overvaluing of your own failure?

Tell God again. Do not give up on God helping you. Try again. Dust those boots off and make a genuine effort one more time. I feel the cheesy phrases coming. Progress, not perfection. Marathon, not a sprint. Put one foot in front of the other.

If it is a past thing, let it go! It is done, over, *finito*. The cross was big enough!

If your secret shame is in the past and it is not something you struggle with anymore, thank God for His faithfulness and deliverance. Remember the pain and celebrate the victory.

We talked about two big things today—pride toward others and unconfessed secret shame. Psalm 51 is believed to be David's heart cry to God after sleeping with Bathsheba and ordering her husband to the front of the battle line to die, all because she got pregnant from his secret sin. God knew. David knew.

Read Psalm 51 in your own Bible, or if this passage is really familiar, it might help you to get a fresh perspective and read The Message, Eugene Peterson's version of it here. (Remember as we talked about the first week, in the last verses, the bulls were the animals sacrificed to pay for wrongdoing.)

Rewrite the verses or the parts of the chapter that stand out to you as a prayer you can say from your heart to God's heart.

> Generous in love—God, give grace! Huge in mercy—wipe out my bad record.
> Scrub away my guilt, soak out my sins in your laundry.
> I know how bad I've been; my sins are staring me down.
> You're the One I've violated, and you've seen it all,
> seen the full extent of my evil.
> You have all the facts before you; whatever you decide about me is fair.
> I've been out of step with you for a long time,
> in the wrong since before I was born.
> What you're after is truth from the inside out.
> Enter me, then; conceive a new, true life.
> Soak me in your laundry and I'll come out clean,
> scrub me and I'll have a snow-white life.
> Tune me in to foot-tapping songs, set these once-broken bones to dancing.
> Don't look too close for blemishes, give me a clean bill of health.

God, make a fresh start in me, shape a Genesis week from the chaos
of my life.
Don't throw me out with the trash, or fail to breathe holiness in me.
Bring me back from gray exile, put a fresh wind in my sails!
Give me a job teaching rebels your ways so the lost can find their
way home.
Commute my death sentence, God, my salvation God,
and I'll sing anthems to your life-giving ways.
Unbutton my lips, dear God; I'll let loose with your praise.
Going through the motions doesn't please you,
a flawless performance is nothing to you.
I learned God-worship when my pride was shattered.
Heart-shattered lives ready for love don't for a moment escape God's
notice.
Make Zion the place you delight in, repair Jerusalem's broken-down
walls.
Then you'll get real worship from us, acts of worship small and large,
Including all the bulls they can heave onto your altar!
(Psalm 51, MSG)

Week Seven, Day Three:
People Pleasing... Looking Out for Number One

Father, help me to concern myself with pleasing You more than the people around me.

While my car was in the shop getting repaired, my husband texted that he would not be able to pick up our son at school. Having lived in Arizona a short time, the few people I could call to help were picking up their own children at other schools. Just before panic set in, I remembered that my twenty-year-old moped from my college days was functional. However embarrassed I was to put on that helmet and head down the road as "that person" slowing down the traffic (remember the speeding tickets in ten states?), my embarrassment did not hold a candle to my absolutely mortified fourteen-year-old son riding away from school on a moped with his mom. He was humiliated, looking every direction for who might see him, worrying about every car and its occupants and what they were witnessing of his existence! Of course being the good mom that I am, I did things like wave and make sure we were in clear view to enjoy the experience all the more!

I remember being fourteen and wanting to look good in front of my peers. With age, people pleasing and wanting to look good in front of others subsides and improves, but I do not think we reach a point that we do not want to be considered valuable by others. Whether a mom or a spouse, you desire your kids and husband to acknowledge your contribution to their lives and "approve" of your methods or results. At work, you might desire recognition for your contribution. At church, you may desire others to respect your opinions or demonstrate value by listening. People pleasing—desiring to be recognized and esteemed—may look different as we age, but it is still present. In light of this honesty, read Matthew 6:1–8 and 16–18.

The Pharisees are, yet again, doing the right things for the wrong reasons, as they wanted to be seen and heard. Motives and the heart can call into question any action. I do not know about you, but I love the way Jesus and scripture often cut straight to the heart of the matter. *Why* are you serving God? *Why* are you praying? *Why* are you at church every Sunday? *Why* are you feeding the poor? Do you do what you do out of a genuine response to God because He first loved you? Are you following that scriptural teaching because you genuinely desire to love God in the way you behave, or is it just about meeting your list of being a Christian or a "good person"? Is it about elevating yourself and making others look on you more favorably?

I find this to be so complicated, because I can at one moment be doing the right thing for the right reason, and then have someone give me a compliment, and my heart in a split second can become about me looking good. I can forget my disciplines of following God. My actions can turn into habit and checklists of good behavior instead of heart engagement with God. Motives complicate all behavior.

Let us refer back to Jesus' example. We saw, in our very first homework assignment, Jesus practice His own private relationship with the Father. He regularly retreated to spend time with Him away from others. In private, there is no audience. Jesus knew this.

Think through this one and be honest as you answer. Do you have a genuine private practice of relationship with God? And if not, why not?

If you do practice your own time alone with God, do you use it as something to "check off" your spiritual to-do list?

Do you see any ways you are straying from loving God and loving others?

Motives relate particularly to public prayer. Do you hesitate to pray because you are concerning yourself with those around you?

When you pray in public, are your words for God or for those around you? In other words, are you wondering about what others might think when you pray, or are you in genuine conversation with God without worrying about their opinion? Close today with a prayer about any of these concepts.

Week Seven, Day Four:
The Heart of the Matter

Father, discern my heart and help me to prioritize what You intend.

This is one of those days that may seem unrelated to prayer. Keep in mind that from our hearts come our actions. If we are not praying or prioritizing prayer, the choices we make reflect what we love and prioritize. Time and again, while in prayer, my heart has been revealed, even changed. A deeply seeded struggle has been revealed. A bad attitude softened. My current priorities realigned. As we look at prayer and our hearts today, keep this in mind.

Read Luke 12:30–34, then continue reading Jesus' words that we began reading yesterday in Matthew 6:19–21. Obviously, Luke and Matthew both recorded this part of Jesus' sermon.

Where is your treasure? Where is your heart?

Luke uses the Greek word for heart twenty-two times in his twenty-four-chapter summary of Jesus' entire life. The Greek word for heart is *kardia* (kar-dee-ah). It can mean the physical organ, but there are many other meanings from *Thayer's Greek and English Lexicon of the New Testament.*[12]

- Denotes the center of all physical and spiritual life.

- The vigor and sense of physical life.

- The center and seat of spiritual life including the soul or mind, as it is the fountain and seat of the thoughts, passions, desires, appetites, purposes,

---

12 Joseph Thayer, *Thayer's Greek and English Lexicon of the New Testament* (Peabody, MA: Hendrickson Publishers, 1986).

endeavors, of the understanding, the faculty and seat of intelligence, of the will and character, of the soul so far as it is affected and stirred in a bad or good way, or the soul as the soul as the seat of sensibilities.

- Of the middle or central or inmost part of anything, even though inanimate.

Remember, your treasure is not financial things alone. Your treasure is whatever matters to you. It is what you treasure. It could be time, talent, relationships, emotions, money, or other things.

"For where your treasure is, there will your heart be also" (Matthew 6:21).

Think beyond just your treasure of money to consider the pieces of your treasure: love, service, talent, and anything you have to give or sacrifice. What do you treasure? Where does all of your heart and money go to? Kelly Minter, in her study *No Other Gods*, talks about how the things we fear are often related to our idols or gods. What is it that strikes fear or worry? What do you think about, financial security, children's success, aging appearance, wanting something? There are so many options!

With years, my heart's focus changes over and over. But evaluating the condition of our hearts by questioning our current priorities of time, love, money, work, and talents can help keep us on course and in line with God's intentions and priorities.

How do you prioritize time for each of the following? Think through what you invest in each and what priority they take in your life.

- Talent

- Work/Service

- Emotions

- Money

- Relationships

Today's homework is short because I want you to spend your time with God praying about this. I first remember hearing a chorus from a song by Keith Green in the 70s that is taken directly from Psalm 51 that we read earlier this week. Whether I need an attitude adjustment, hyperfocusing on a failure, or I just need a reminder that God has to be the One to renew my spirit and restore my joy, these words have reached my heart many times. If you know the melody, sing it to God in your mind or out loud. If not, pray the words. Take time to be still and know that He is God! Get quiet long enough to listen. He might have something to say back to you. Listen._

As you do this, evaluate your heart and the things you wrote or considered on the previous page. Where is your heart? Where are your priorities of time, money, and gifting?

Give this at least ten minutes. (That is not long . . . you can do it . . . yes, you can. Set a timer if you need to.) Ask God to show you where your heart is, and ask Him to do this.

"Create in Me a Clean Heart" by Keith Green[13]

"Create in me a clean heart, oh God,
and renew a right spirit within me.
Cast me not away from thy presence, Oh Lord.
Take not thy Holy Spirit from me."
Restore unto me the joy of thy salvation,
and renew a right spirit within me."

Journal your thoughts or prayer here.

---

13   Lyrics taken verbatim from Psalm 51:10–12a, The Holy Bible King James Version

Week Eight:
Adoration

Teaching Session Eight: Seeing Who He Is

1. Adoration is not _____.

2. If you want to be an imitator of God, you must _____ He
   is _____. Ephesians 5:1

3. To believe He is deserving, you have to _____ who He is.

4. Knowing who He is _____ your behavior, as well as
   your _____ to _____
   _____.
   Jeremiah 29:11; Psalm 146:1–7

5. Grasping the _____ of God will help you
   _____ His plan when it _____ with your plan.

6. Write notes as you watch this segment: *How Great Is Our God,* Louie
   Giglio

   _____
   _____
   _____
   _____
   _____
   _____

Are your life circumstances trumping your experience of the reality and person
of God?
Hebrews 13:15; 1 Peter 2:9

We must KNOW the _____ of God and _____ of God to achieve the _____ accomplishment He intends for us!

Before you read this, please do not be intimidated by its length. I want you to choose the part or pieces of this passage that stand out in your heart and mind. I could not narrow this down for you, as I think the context is so powerful. Isaiah is speaking, so please be prayerful that God would give you understanding to grasp His magnitude.

Memory Verse

"In the year that King Uzziah died I saw the Lord sitting upon a throne, high and lifted up; and the train of his robe filled the temple. Above him stood the seraphim. Each had six wings: with two he covered his face, and with two he covered his feet, and with two he flew. And one called to another and said: 'Holy, holy, holy is the LORD of hosts; the whole earth is full of his glory!' And the foundations of the thresholds shook at the voice of him who called, and the house was filled with smoke. And I said: 'Woe is me! For I am lost; for I am a man of unclean lips, and I dwell in the midst of a people of unclean lips; for my eyes have seen the King, the LORD of hosts!'" (Isaiah 6:1–5).

Write out the verse(s) you want to focus on this week in the translation you prefer.

Let me start this week by saying it will be a little different homework-wise. I want to stress that our goal is to incorporate adoration of God into our everyday life experience. Next time you are in a church service, when it comes time to sing with the band or choir, close your eyes and "rest" in the words and message. Notice when the words are not about you, just about God's character. Let the words wash over you in a way that your heart and mind engages. It might help you to not sing, but be still and know that He is God. Do whatever helps you experience or sense the Holy Spirit. Throughout your week, notice the beauty of His creation. Find music that helps you elevate God in your heart and mind. Look for opportunities to adore our most awe-inspiring God.

Week Eight, Day One:
Altars and Celebrations, Remembering and Thanksgiving

Father, help me to cultivate gratitude by remembering Your works in my life.

When I was a child, Dad drove me to school if Mom was otherwise obligated. Occasionally, with five loud, chatty kids in the car, he would drive right past the exit for the school. My dad is an extremely intelligent business man, who at that time was running a large company's multi-million-dollar portfolio. I still tease him about this, as I had the good fortune to inherit his memory.

So, just like the Israelites in scripture, I do not remember things God has done for me, and I head out on my own road. I see God's grace in the way He recognized human forgetfulness. He had our heroes of scripture build altars to remember and He established holidays (Passover, Feast of Booths, even the Sabbath) so His people would not forget His faithfulness and history with them.

How do you remember God's faithfulness to you? In recent years, I chose a particular Bible with larger margins, and I marked certain passages that had significance at different times. I write the circumstances or event, how God spoke to me in a particular way surrounding that passage, and I date it. The most significant lessons stand out in such a way that I can tell you where I was sitting, likening it to those historical moments like 9/11 when our world was shaken. These are many times God shook my world. Whether it was a revelation of poor character on my part, direction for my future, or just being awe-struck by our awe-inspiring God, these margin notes commemorate my history with Him. When I thumb through those pages, I am reminded of God's faithfulness.

How do you, or how can you, begin to build your altars to remember God? If you do not have a system, I suggest starting one.

Attempt to differentiate between appreciating God's character versus being thankful for God's work. This is the difference between adoration and thanksgiving. Sometimes they are so intertwined it is hard to differentiate' other times it is very clear. The rest of the week we will be focused on who God is and His character. Today we practice both.

Write either your God story as a narrative, choosing three times you sensed Him in a special way, or use specific things God has done in your life. Take time to remember and celebrate what He did for you and thank Him for it.

Week Eight, Day Two:
Adoring God through Scripture

Father, teach my heart to genuinely adore You.

Webster's defines adoration as the act of paying homage to a divine being; worship.

As I began my walk with Jesus, adoration eluded me. When we sang songs or read scriptures of the lofty characteristics of God, I did not connect to the dialogue. If you are there, give yourself grace for the process God is doing in your life. Please do not let it discourage you from doing the homework. These exercises may help, but God will help whether the exercises do or not. Grace, grace, and more grace, as scripture says.

The Psalms carry a theme of adoration in so many places, but today I want us to look at a few chapters in Job. In the first passage, Job was getting lectured by his friend who was berating him for his lack of faith. God walloped them both, and hopefully us too, with His interruption in this conversation. Attempt to acknowledge, by writing down, all you see of God's character and His work as you read this text. Read Job from 38:1 all the way through 40:5.

Adore our amazing and awe-inspiring God!

If there is amazement in your heart, write it here. If not, pray about your process of learning adoration. Write it out as a prayer here.

Week Eight, Day Three:
Practice

Week Eight, Day Four:
More Practice

Father, may I habitually practice adoration in my life.

Start each day, if you have computer access, by watching a YouTube video of a worship song that doesn't center on you, but on God's character. It might show my age, but I love Carrie Underwood singing "How Great Thou Art." Focus on God instead of the music. If no computer access, listen to a song about who God is.

After this, do one or more of the following exercises:

- Play the alphabet game and try to come up with a characteristic of God for as many letters as you can. Be in a posture of adoring Him.

- Go on a walk, run, or bike ride and look around you at God's beautiful creation. In your heart and mind, connect your heart to Him and talk to Him about it. Do this for at least fifteen minutes.

- Read one or more of the Psalms in chapters 91–95. Meditate on the words.

- Get completely still and quiet. (Set a timer if you will struggle.) Close your eyes and review your God story and experiences.

- Read out loud Job 38–39. Note the characteristics of God.

- Get alone and sing or quote a favorite worship song or read a Psalm that focuses on God's character out loud as a prayer to Him. Remember—He made your voice!

One of my prayer partners in New England would pray in "color." She would grab colored pencils and doodle her prayers. Try this. You can write words or draw or just doodle. Just remember that we are focusing on who God is to adore Him.

Read Isaiah 6:1–5. Envision yourself in Isaiah's place witnessing this amazing scene.

Make up your own expression of adoration. Practice it and tell your group about it next week.

Week Nine:
Holy Spirit

Teaching Session Nine:
Recognizing the Holy Spirit Inside Us

1. We want a _____.
   Fleece in Judges 6:37
   Remember there is no resolution in Psalm 88

2. Being "filled with the Holy Spirit" is repeated time after time in the New Testament from people who knew Jesus. Does this mean, at certain times, they have a greater _____ of the Holy Spirit?
   _____ (Luke 4)

   Barnabas (Acts 11:24)

   _____ (Acts 6:4–8)

   Paul (Acts 14:9)

3. Ways we can participate

   _____

   Spend time with God to recognize His voice.

   Ask (Memory Verse, Luke 11:13)

   Do not _____ the Holy Spirit.
   Ephesians 4:29–31; Acts 7:51–52
   _____

   Romans 8:5–7; Acts 5:32; Isaiah 63:10

   _____ your will. "Not my will, but thine."

   The Holy Spirit is _____ for You! Romans 8:26

Watch for the results:

- Fruit of the Spirit, Galatians 5:22–23
- Gifts of the Spirit, 1 Corinthians 12

Memory Verse

"If you then, who are evil, know how to give good gifts to your children, how much more will the heavenly Father give the Holy Spirit to those who ask him!" (Luke 11:13).

Once again, write out this memory verse in the translation of your choice.

Ask God to help you see how this applies to you this week!

We have completed the list from that first week of how Jesus practiced prayer. Even though we completed the list, an event occurred as Jesus died that dramatically impacts our prayer life. The Holy Spirit was released. I would be remiss to close a study on prayer without addressing this. The Bible tells us that the Holy Spirit intercedes for us, and understanding this Spirit enhances our prayer journey.

As we are doing a study of prayer, the questions repeatedly ask you to be still and spend time with God. I apologize that it feels repetitive. But unfortunately, learning lifestyle prayer requires practice just like any other skill we want to acquire. Do not lose sight of the goal due to what might seem like monotonous steps.

Week Nine, Day One:
The Holy Spirit and Luke

Father, help me this week to grasp the Holy Spirit and its significance for more depth in my prayer life.

We are spending this week on the Holy Spirit. Depending on where you attend church and the perspective God has given you over time, these words elicit different things. Starting with scripture, of course, we move into determining how you personally can relate better to this amazing Spirit inside of us, as believers in Christ.

We are focusing more heavily on Luke's story of Jesus. Let's look at how and when Luke references the Holy Spirit. Read the following scriptures from Luke and note, if anything, about how the Holy Spirit stands out to you. Notice particularly if the Holy Spirit is performing a function or connecting in prayer.

Regarding Jesus' coming:
1:15 (verses 14–16, about John the Baptist)

1:35 (verses 34–36, to Mary about Jesus' conception)

1:41 (Elizabeth, John the Baptist's mom)

1:67 (Zechariah, John the Baptist's dad)

2:25–27 (Simeon) What was revealed to Simeon? How?

Regarding Jesus Himself:
3:16
3:22
4:1
4:14
10:21
11:13
12:10–12

This week is scripture heavy, but I really want us to have a full picture surrounding Jesus' life and teaching about the Holy Spirit:

Read Jesus' words from John:

> "Whoever believes in me, as the Scripture has said, 'Out of his heart will flow rivers of living water.' Now this he said about the Spirit, whom those who believed in him were to receive, for as yet the Spirit had not been given, because Jesus was not yet glorified." (John 7:38–39)

> "These things I have spoken to you while I am still with you. But the Helper, the Holy Spirit, whom the Father will send in my name, he will teach you all things and bring to your remembrance all that I have said to you." (John 14:25–26)

You know I love the memory part. Thank goodness He elicits memories to remind me of His faithfulness and lessons I need to retrieve from my storage banks. Some of you have heard these things over and over, and for others it is brand-new, but regardless of where you are, write down anything that stood out to you from these scriptures about the Holy Spirit. Here are some questions if nothing stood out for you today.

What did you see in these verses?

Do the words *Holy Spirit* strike you in any particular way?

What fear, if any, do you have surrounding this concept?

Write or speak your prayer here. Ask God to help you understand or learn something new about the Holy Spirit during these next few days.

Nerd Alert

Do you remember the first week's teaching session about the Holy Spirit, the Holy of Holies, and the significance of the cross? At the moment of Jesus' death, recorded in Matthew 27:51, the veil separating the Spirit of God from humanity tore from top to bottom. God's Spirit was no longer confined to the Holy of Holies because Jesus' spilled blood had completed and fulfilled the blood requirement once and for all.

Read Leviticus 16 to see God's specific instructions to Aaron for the necessity and details of blood requirements for the High Priest to pass the veil. Aaron's two sons died because they did not follow the instructions.

Here are Matthew Henry's comments* about this passage in Leviticus:

> Since the priests have been warned by the death of Nadab and Abihu to approach God with reverence and godly fear, directions are here given how the nearest approach might be made . . . Within the veil none must ever come but the high priest only, and he but one day in the year. But see

> what a blessed change is made by the Gospel of Christ; all good Christians now have boldness to enter into the Holy of Holies, through the veil, every day (Hebrews 10:19, 20); and we come boldly (not as Aaron must, with fear and trembling) to the throne of grace, or mercy seat (Heb. 4:16) . . . Now therefore we are welcome to come at all times into the Holy Place "not made with hands." In the past Aaron could not come near "at all times," lest he die; we now must come near "at all times," that we may live. It is [keeping our] distance only that is our death. (Matthew Henry, A Commentary).

> Freed to live among humans because of Jesus' spilled blood, the Holy Spirit still unleashes and empowers us today. The cross set the stage for the events we will see in Acts 2 tomorrow.

> *Matthew Henry, *A Commentary* (Nashville, TN: Thomas Nelson, 1997).

Week Nine, Day Two:
The Holy Spirit Poured Out

Father, help me to recognize the Holy Spirit's movement in and through me.

Let's complete the story from yesterday. Read Acts 2:1–13.

The Holy Spirit was given to the disciples. What an amazing sight! I so wish I could go back in time and visit this amazing moment! If you continue reading the story of the acts of the disciples, you become an eyewitness to how Christianity began to spread across the world at that time. But I digress, back to the Holy Spirit. Did you catch yesterday that Jesus said those who believed in Him would be given the Holy Spirit? Let's visit one other verse in case you need another confirmation.

Read 1 Corinthians 6:19. Though this passage is actually discussing sexual immorality, it is clear to say the Holy Spirit is in you.

Do you recognize the Holy Spirit inside of you?

Read John 3:7–9 if you struggle to see the Holy Spirit inside of you. If you are a believer in Christ, trust that the Spirit is in you. You can look back at Day One to see which individuals Jesus defined to be given the Spirit of God. If you are unsure you are a believer, seek God in prayer about this, and talk to someone at your church. The Bible repeatedly says, "Seek and you will find." If you earnestly look for God, He will show Himself to you. Know that He is not playing a game of hide and seek.

Put a marker or a finger on this passage, as the Nerd Alert will bring you back here. Read 1 Corinthians 12:7–12 about the ways the Holy Spirit will manifest itself in you. I know we have talked about spiritual gifts before, but here we see their origination from the Spirit.

Do you know what your spiritual gifting is? If so, list it here.

Remember us talking about passions? What are your spiritual passions?

Your gifting is so important because it will be where you find productivity for the Kingdom of Christ. If you know your spiritual gift, take time to pray right now for sensitivity to the Holy Spirit's direction. (Set that timer if you need it.) If you do not know, pray for the Holy Spirit to direct you to learn what your gifting is.

Journal any thoughts about your personal gifting.

Nerd Alert

In 1 Corinthians 12, we see a specific list of the spiritual gifts. Remember that Paul did not split his letter into chapters and verses. That was done later for us to be able to reference the material. Paul begins a discussion on spiritual gifting, which continues in chapters 13 and 14. If you have time, read these three chapters as one message right now.

You probably are familiar with chapter 13, as it is known as the love chapter. But do not miss that Paul, right in the middle of his conversation about gifts, includes a beautiful illustration of love. Paul is speaking about gifts of prophecy, administration, service, teaching, tongues, healing, and more, yet he stops to reiterate that love is the most important of all before he continues. He stresses that the body is to work together and reminds us passionately and eloquently about love's importance.

I have a theory. Paul's plea for love in the middle of his lecture on gifts could confirm this theory. I believe that we have entire churches and denominations with members who have similar giftings and passions. Our corporate thinking becomes that every believer should be doing what God has gifted or led us to do, and "they" (all other churches or believers) are doing it wrong. Scripture interpretation and perspective then becomes tainted with predetermined points and passions and is used as a whipping tool for "them." In other words, we use scripture to elevate ourselves because of our callings or giftedness.

Here are some examples: My friend with a passion for evangelism is appalled by anyone not sharing the gospel. Her scripture focus could be the Great Commission, Acts, or the story of the watchtower. My friend with outstanding faith considers anyone to be downcast who doesn't have her positive outlook. Her scripture focus could be the Hall of Faith from Hebrews, miraculous healing, or belief teachings. My friend with an extra dose of discernment struggles with those not following clear teaching on righteousness. She could see from any passage the "rules" of living. My friend with a passion for taking care of the poor wants to bring an end to American extravagances, thus annoyed by believers with nice cars or big houses. Her scripture focus could be on the sheep and the goats, communal living of the New Testament followers, or Micah's call to fairness. My friend who is a mercy giver wants to love everyone, but she can get annoyed by seeing any one of them as judgmental. Her scripture focus could be on the passages about grace and the Pharisees elevating themselves because of their "accurate theology." My gift is teaching, and I have talked about how I get crazy when scripture is quoted out of context. My scripture focus is on passages calling us to dependence on the power of God with contemplation.

God calls us to evangelism, faith, discernment of truth, feeding the poor, mercy, and teaching. Do you see how our passions, giftedness, and following particular scripture can be used to elevate ourselves via our God-given giftedness or passion? Paul pleads for effective functioning in all of God's purposes by way of love.

And the greatest of these is love.

Week Nine, Day Three:

Interceding with the Spirit

Father, open my eyes to the Holy Spirit's functioning.

Isn't our God amazing? A friend texted me that she was going through a hard time. I took a little time to pray through my response and sent her three scriptures that stood out in my heart and mind. One was not a commonly discussed passage. As only the Holy Spirit can do, she ended up reading the exact same verse in a book she was currently reading. Over 31,000 verses in the Bible, and this particular day, her two exposures to scripture were the same. (Just in case you have any appreciation for numbers, I had given her three verses, which meant the likelihood was 0.000096 of 1 percent chance!) Only the Holy Spirit can do that, and this is often how the Spirit works in my life. I am not predicting or presuming a particular visual imprint of the Holy Spirit with your unique gifting or how often it will happen, but I am predicting if you have believed on Christ, I am confident the Holy Spirit will work in and through you.

Let's review one scripture we have already seen* as we read about the Holy Spirit functions, aside from the gifting we discussed yesterday. Write beside these scriptures the function listed there. It pains me because I wish we could go through every single scripture and function, but there are just too many, so we will cover a few here. Cover as many as you can.

Luke 12:11–12

John 6:63

*John 14:26 (reviewed on Day One)

John 15:26

John 16:13

Acts 1:8

Romans 5:5

Romans 8:26–27

The Holy Spirit is multitasking beyond what most of us can comprehend, and it is not even all inclusive. He gives us gifting, helps us in our weaknesses, intercedes for us, makes us witnesses of the gospel, gives us truth and testifies to Jesus, gives us love, teaches us, helps us to remember, gives us words to say, and downright gives us life. Now that is multitasking!

My multitasking looks something like this: working on multiple projects for church, hosting a sixth-grade group of girls for a sleepover, thinking through my lunch plan as well as a medicine choice for my son's cough, running a load of laundry, and watching *Mission Impossible 3* with that sick boy. Yet, the Holy Spirit multitasks for every single person who believes. This is awe inspiring and definitely more than I can handle.

Knowing our limitations, I want you to focus on the characteristic(s) that stand out to you right now. Trust this very Spirit we are studying to reveal to your heart in this moment what you need to grasp today.

What Holy Spirit functions stand out?

Once again, practice being still. Listen. Journal your thoughts. Pray that the Holy Spirit would guide you.

Week Nine, Day Four:

Allowing the Spirit to Comfort, Move, and Guide You

Father, may my heart recognize Your Holy Spirit's direction with clarity.

When my father was diagnosed with cancer shortly after we moved to Massachusetts, I was devastated. For the first time in my life, I did not live a drivable distance to my parents. My brother had died just a few months before, and as an only child, I wanted to be present to help my parents as they navigated something so difficult. As my pellet-stove fire burned in our beautiful New England sunroom overlooking the lake, I laid out on the brick floor to pray. I sobbed and pleaded for Dad to not be taken from us yet. I pleaded for my kids to at least be able to know him long enough to remember him.

I flew home to Memphis to be there after his surgery during his hospitalization. While I was in the hospital room, the doctor came in and told us that of the nineteen lymph nodes removed with his colon, cancer was in thirteen of them. This was a death sentence from any human perspective, and I knew it.

I attended a mom's prayer group when Dad was diagnosed. Before I had gone home for the surgery, a Spirit-filled pray-er friend of mine had prayed for him. Imagine this scene. My friend was deaf in one ear, and had overall poor hearing, so she prayed loudly. Midway through her prayer, she put her hand on my leg, looked at me, and said, "Sandi, God just told me that He will heal your dad." I have to tell you that I hesitated. I am not even certain those were her exact words, but the message was clear. We were deep in prayer at the moment, and I was not sure how to react, but I was hopeful.

Just weeks after that moment, I found myself listening to the doctor's report in Dad's hospital room. I struggled for days with my faith versus the medical reality of our current situation. One minute I was begging for that predicted miracle to be true—in a heartbeat I would be praying that I would

151

know how to "walk this,"—and the next minute I was fuming that God allowed someone to tell me he would be healed when he obviously had not been!

As my Holy-Spirit-filled friend had predicted, the doctor declared my dad "cancer free" six years ago, six months after the prayer time. He did follow medical protocol and have chemotherapy, but I know in my heart that his cancer did not spread because he was healed by God's intervention. Our God is in the business of miracles.

The question for us today is how did my friend know or recognize the Holy Spirit in her prayer that day? How do we become people who recognize the Holy Spirit at work? God definitely speaks His truth to us through others, but I want to be in tune to Him and His Spirit in a way that I am sensitive to hearing and believing.

We all want a formula, don't we? Though in the teaching segment, we reviewed some pointers from scripture. More often than not, hearing the Holy Spirit does not function in the way our human minds and efforts work. So I will not specify a five-step process.

We could revisit specific gifting in 1 Corinthians 14, but our goal needs to be for each of us to recognize what the Holy Spirit intends for our ears. We saw in Luke where the Holy Spirit filled Zechariah and he prophesied. We saw that Jesus was "filled with the Holy Spirit," which led him to the wilderness to be tempted, and then led Him as He began His public ministry. We saw the disciples healing people and speaking in different languages in Acts 2.

As the Bible says in a few places, physical healing cannot be assumed. Jesus spoke of the man who was not sick because of what he had done but because God would be glorified. First Corinthians 14 says clearly that we do not all have the gift of healing, nor do we all have the gift of tongues. But it also says the Holy Spirit resides in believers of Christ. Jesus said, "My sheep hear my voice, and I know them, and they follow me" (John 10:27). Pray today that you will know the voice of God. Pray today that He will begin to teach you. Come on, I do not mean to just read the words—pray. Right now—pray these things to Him.

Set your timer and let's end this week with being still and knowing that He is God. Take whatever time you can spare—ten minutes, fifteen, or more. Ask God to reveal Himself to you. Ask God to reveal the Holy Spirit to you.

Week Ten:
Having Faith

Teaching Session Ten: Pray Believingly

1. Do you _____?

2. Almost every miracle Jesus performed, He said, "According to your _____."

3. Jesus said, "If you ask _____ in My name, I will do it, _____ the Father will be glorified." John 14:13–14

4. Tell God the _____ about your _____. Evaluate your _____.

5. The act of _____ is an act of _____.
   • Do not forget you can pray the "_____ my _____" prayer.
   • Do not forget the _____.
   • Do not be _____.
   • Do not forget _____.
   John the Baptist, Matthew 11:2–7

6. Submit to His _____, and _____ what He _____.

7. Keep on _____ and _____.

8. Think _____! Ask _____!

ASK exceedingly abundantly beyond anything we can think or imagine. (Ephesians 3:20)

Remember, we serve a BIG GOD!

Memory Verse

"And without faith it is impossible to please him, for whoever would draw near to God must believe that he exists and that he rewards those who seek him"
(Hebrews 11:6).

Write out this verse in the translation of your choice:

Week Ten, Day One:

Where Are You on the Faith Spectrum?

Father, reveal my strengths and weaknesses in faith today.

My children are two very different people. My daughter sees life through rose-colored glasses. No matter what the circumstance, she has a positive take. My son, on the other hand, sees life through high magnification glasses with extra focus on what needs to be changed. Each of them work diligently to help "correct" their sibling's incorrect perspective to view life through his or her lens. There is no time this was more evident than when we were looking at houses in New England. (Keep in mind we were moving there from our "Dallas palace.")

We were looking at a home in the foreclosure process. To say its upkeep was in a deficit understates the condition significantly. After walking through the house, our (then) eight-year-old boy announced, "This is a horrible house. It is tiny. It is very ugly. It stinks and is moldy. My room would be much smaller. The swimming pool is black and icky."

Our (then) five-year-old daughter's reaction was very different. "It has a huge yard and a pool. There will be ducks in the lake! That long driveway will be a great place to ride bikes. It has a pink room for me!"

All those statements were factually accurate (except tiny, but it was a child who moved from Texas). We bought that house. What they chose to focus on determined their perspective.

Perspectives on what having faith looks like, particularly in prayer, vary just as dramatically as my children's perspectives differed on our home in Massachusetts that day. Faith in this context does not refer to our overall religious belief system but our confidence that God will actually do what we are asking.

Some people invest their time in prayer, sometimes for years, pleading for physical healing. Some, as we have discussed, do not mention sin or their sickness and focus on positive speaking, believing faith looks like taking their mind off the hardships to focus on God's power. Some believers' faith looks more like endurance to believe God through the suffering. They might not even ask for their desires because faith in God's sovereignty means their desires always fall under God's plan. They do not speak what they actually want, believing God's plan will happen anyway. Some believers' prayers focus on scripture, and their prayer life is words of scripture spoken to God over and over. They use their faith in the truth of scripture to retrain their minds in communication with God. Many of us at different times and different situations fit into any or all of these categories.

All those different scenarios might make your head spin. Are you like me and forget what a conversation is about? This entire week, our focus is on how our faith or belief in God to respond to our requests affects *whether* we ask, *how* we ask, and *what* we ask.

"Prayer faith" is our belief that God will actually do what we are asking. How does your belief in God to respond affect the following?

If you ask . . .

How you ask . . .

What you ask . . .

Our challenge this week is to determine where our belief in God to answer prayer is strong or weak, to evaluate it honestly, and to bring it in line with God's truth and a genuine practice of believing God to do the extraordinary.

Do you know that you have the gift of faith, healing, or miracles?

First Corinthians 12:9–10 lays these out as clear spiritual giftings. However, I do not have one of these giftings, so if you are like me, skip to the next paragraph. If this is your gifting, how does it affect your prayer life? And how can you more effectively use these gifts in and through the discipline of prayer?

The rest of us can think about the following questions, though we will not answer now. Some of them, we will put pen to paper later. We will close today repeating these questions and give you time and space to contemplate them.

- Where is your faith strong and where do you doubt God?

- Do you believe God to ask more for physical things or spiritual things?

- What type of requests do you not ask because you believe it falls in the "Sovereign God" category?

- Do you use "God's will" as an excuse to not speak your mind to Him?

- Do you persist in asking for things you really desire?

- Do you speak with confidence telling God what things He is to accomplish in your life?

- Are you on the brink of being downright whiny because you will not let it go with your persistent asking?

- Do you wonder when it is time to stop asking?

Is your challenge to even allow yourself to speak the negative, fearing it will get a grip on you? These are not easy questions. And many of them do not have "right" answers. I want clear-cut answers. I want God to say, "Yes, I am healing you via this doctor or by way of a miracle on this date." "Yes, your sister will recognize Jesus as Savior on September 24, 2014." "No, he is going to die and it will happen on . . ." "I am going to make you wait thirty-three years, and we will be working through your unhealthy connection to food until you are XX years old. I will accomplish this freedom by way of many struggles in relationship, weight changes, and heart-wrenching losses." "No, you must ask five more times, and then I will give it to you."

God has given me many clear-cut answers to prayer, but they haven't usually come in this black-and-white format, so how do we keep believing and praying? What does believing, praying, knowing God knows best, and yet asking Him to do exceedingly abundantly beyond what we can think look like?

This is an age-old debate: God's will and authority as sovereign versus God's answers to prayer. If God already has a plan, how does my praying make a difference anyway? I do not have that comfortable, clear-cut formula, my friends. And this debate persists throughout the millennia.

My experience has been that sometimes God uses my asking to completely change my heart to see the situation as He does. Prayer changes me in these instances. I know there have been many times the person has been healed, the person has accepted Jesus, and I have experienced freedom from long-term sin. We read story after story in scripture where God was set to do one thing, and someone pleaded with God with heartfelt boldness, and God reacted. The reality is that we will never know without God's direct revelation which one is happening, and obsessing over debate is nonproductive.

Both things are in scripture. So we walk in faith trusting that when God commanded us to pray and gave us an example of prayer, it was for a reason. We choose to believe and trust Him in spite of what the answer is, and we admit our heart honestly as we respond with respect and obedience. What was our original thought and definition? Faith in prayer is believing that God will respond.

The next couple of days, we will review scriptures and concepts as we attempt to see where God wants to refine and improve our faith. Forgive me if this feels like you are sitting in the chaise in a psychiatrist's office. But recognizing our personalities and predispositions aids our abilities to discern our hearts regarding which truths and falsehoods surround our personal belief and doubt.

Bring this to Jesus. Ask Him to reveal the questions He wants you to ask yourself surrounding faith this week. You can journal your prayer here. Or if you want to reread these questions to give some clarity to this prayer, do so.

Where is your faith strong and where do you doubt God?

Do you believe God to ask more for physical things or spiritual things?

What type of requests do you not ask for because you believe it falls in the "Sovereign God" category?

Do you use "God's will" as an excuse to not speak your mind to Him?

Do you persist in asking for things you really desire?

Do you speak with confidence telling God what things He is to accomplish in your life?

Are you on the brink of being downright whiny because you will not let it go with your persistent asking?

Do you wonder when it is time to stop asking?

Is your challenge to even allow yourself to speak the negative, fearing it will get a grip on you?

Week Ten, Day Two:
According to Your Faith

Father, grow my faith, belief, and trust in You.

We read this passage during Week Two when we talked about worrying, but isn't worrying a direct reflection of a lack of faith? Re-read James' words from The Message:

> "If you don't know what you're doing, pray to the Father. He loves to help. You'll get his help, and won't be condescended to when you ask for it. Ask boldly, believingly, without a second thought. People who 'worry their prayers' are like wind-whipped waves. Don't think you're going to get anything from the Master that way, adrift at sea, keeping all your options open" (James 1:5–8, MSG).

I find these words to be so powerful. Have you "worried your prayers"? Worried many a prayer, I have. (Did you just hear Yoda in that sentence structure, or just me, it is?)

There is a repeated pattern in Jesus' words when He heals people. He says phrases like, "According to your faith," "Your faith has healed you," and "You have great faith." Jesus clearly correlated faith with the miraculous.

This next one could be painful. "And he did not do many mighty works there because of their unbelief" (Matthew 13:58).

The NIV says "And he did not do many miracles because of their lack of faith." Remember that you only need faith the size of a mustard seed in believing God. A mustard seed. Have you ever seen a mustard seed? It would fit inside this small letter o! What would Jesus do "according to your faith"?

Remember that James said, "You do not have, because you do not ask" (4:2b). Specifically how does your prayer life reflect this faith? Do you ask? And what do you ask?

I have heard Beth Moore say many times, "You believe little because you see little. And you see little because you believe little." Do you believe in God to answer prayer for accomplishing?

On the next page, rate your believing and praying. First, mark your confidence level that God will give you what you are asking for, from doubt to complete confidence. You are not rating what you know God can do, but what you believe God will do in response to your prayer.

Table 1

	Doubt									Complete Confidence
My prayer for salvation	1	2	3	4	5	6	7	8	9	10
God will answer what I ask	1	2	3	4	5	6	7	8	9	10
God will bring me the money I need	1	2	3	4	5	6	7	8	9	10
God will change in me the things I ask	1	2	3	4	5	6	7	8	9	10
God will heal my sickness	1	2	3	4	5	6	7	8	9	10
God will heal my addiction/bad behavior	1	2	3	4	5	6	7	8	9	10
God will keep me safe	1	2	3	4	5	6	7	8	9	10
God will use my talents	1	2	3	4	5	6	7	8	9	10
God will change others	1	2	3	4	5	6	7	8	9	10
God will bring salvation to others	1	2	3	4	5	6	7	8	9	10
God will keep those I love safe	1	2	3	4	5	6	7	8	9	10
God will heal those I love	1	2	3	4	5	6	7	8	9	10

Repeat this exercise using a different mark or color by replacing the scale range to be from never (1) to very often (10). Mark how often you pray about each of these things.

My pastor recently talked about that mustard seed. He talked about how often we think we need to muster up some more faith. Jesus was making the point with the mustard seed that it is not how much faith we have, but Who we believe meets our needs. Is our faith in ourselves or in God? If you and I trust in ourselves instead of our God, we won't ask. If we believe it is coming from God, we will ask.

What was your correlation between how often you pray and where you are more confident in God's answer?

Forgive the math geek here, but if you had an inverse relationship between complete confidence and how often you pray, you might be worrying your prayers and putting your confidence in yourself instead of God. In other words, if the places you are less confident in God's answer are the places you pray the most, it is possible that you are worried because you are not confident in God's participation.

Are your higher ratings the places you more often are able to see God at work? Or do you pray more in the areas you doubt Him?

Are there any other correlations you would like to note?

Jesus' repeated words throughout Luke regarding the miraculous were, "According to your faith, it shall be done to you." From this exercise, hopefully we see some areas where we need our belief to move to being in God.

If this exercise did not reveal your heart in any particular area, just pray that God would remind you of those areas and topics where you think you "worry your prayers." I wish I could sit down with each one of you and talk through those areas that we worry our prayers. I worry my prayers about those babies God gave me who are now teenagers. Choosing to exercise my trust in God with them challenges me greatly.

What area(s) of your life do you struggle to exercise faith? Journal and pray about it here.

Week Ten, Day Three:
Getting Past Our Minds to God's

Father, help my unbelief.

Unbelief happens often in the places we function the best. We can depend on ourselves in those areas, right?

In today's culture, we have so many sources for accurate information. I love information. I love intellectual Christian authors who research and review the physical evidence that supports Christianity. Reading books about intellectual atheists who came to Christ or books expounding upon archeology and evidence that support our Bible thrill my soul. Authors like C. S. Lewis, Josh McDowell, Tim Kellar, and Lee Stroebel write about logic and evidence.

But God does not always operate in our logic, does He? Let's review some Bible events:

- Joshua worked diligently, spent years gathering weapons and preparing his soldiers for battle to skillfully defeat the Canaanites.

- Well, no. Actually, God had them walk around the city, playing trumpets and screaming.

- Gideon took his army of 30,000 in to storm the Midianites.

- Well, no. Actually, God made him decrease the army to three hundred and spread out around the city with no weapon, just lamps.

- David, the strongest and best-armored soldier, used the best shield and sword to defeat Goliath.

- Well, no. Actually, he was the smallest and youngest and went out with a slingshot and some pebbles.

- Jesus Christ came to earth and established himself on a throne with pomp and circumstance to save the kingdom of God.

- Well, no. Actually, He lived as a carpenter and was brutally murdered to save humanity by dying on a cross.

What does this tell us about our logic, our strength, and our plans?

What can you do to know when your strength is appropriate or when your plan is not God's? (Hint: The focus of this study is . . .)

Our logic, strength, and plans are often not going to be in natural alignment with God's plan. Knowing God's Word helps to discern our actions, but His Word, as amazing and awe inspiring as it is, will not direct specifics for every situation. Whether to move or not to move, with which believer to build deeper relationships, which job to take, when to exercise grace or discipline in parenting, when to retire, or where to retire. We make so many decisions.

We must know God's Word and submerse our hearts and minds in it. But there will be some specifics to do, what seem completely off our human map, that can only be directed by the Holy Spirit through prayer. And sadly, a big obstacle to our ability to trust in God or see His direction is often our own intellect. Created by God, the very brain He gave us can become our own demise in faith.

How have you experienced God's plan running counter to the way you would plan the events of your life?

How has your plan and the use of your intellect impeded your faith to trust in His plan?

There was no right answer to those last two questions. Responding with faith and trust to difficult circumstances demands confidence in His character, wisdom, and plan. Demonstrating and walking in His plan sometimes mean we ignore our human conclusion. Let's review what God thinks of those who operate in their own wisdom. Check out what Paul wrote in his first letter to the church in Corinth.

> For the foolishness of God is wiser than men, and the weakness of God is stronger than men. For consider your calling, brothers: not many of you were wise according to worldly standards, not many were powerful, not many were of noble birth. But God chose what is foolish in the world to shame the wise; God chose what is weak in the world to shame the strong; (1 Corinthians 1:25–27)

The stumbling block to us believing, trusting, and having faith in God's logic, strength, and plan can be our human wisdom. The Amplified Version includes the phrase "[that has its source in] God" regarding wisdom. Do you have your source in God?

Can you see a correlation between faith, prayer, and your direction or choices in life?

What intellectual concepts of today and our culture might corrupt your personal faith?

One of my dearest friends adopted three precious, little girls. She already had three children of her own and one adopted. That equals seven children. In addition, her husband changed his career from an outrageously successful developer to a church manager. Their income was literally cut in half. Many of their friends and family could only see the hardship and insanity of responsibility they had assumed. We have all "worried our prayers" for them at times. But God called. They answered. God's plan did not look like the financial comfort of two and half children with a beautiful house. God's plan looked like seven children (four adopted), a chicken coop (that's another story!), a cat, a garden, and my dear friend gaining blessings she never knew she would desire. Living faith means those words we casually toss around from Ephesians of "exceedingly, abundantly beyond anything we ask or think" take on a completely different meaning.

My friends could have at any point allowed human wisdom of financial stability, "margin" in life, or focus on their biological children to stop these adoptions. Some would have even applauded them for this wisdom. But there are four children whose lives will be forever changed!

My calling from God is not to adopt children, but what God calls me to do does not comfortably flow in human thinking either. So what do you think "exceedingly, abundantly beyond anything you can ask or think" might mean for something you should do right now?

Pray and believe.
Let Him direct and whisk you away on the adventure of your lifetime!

Week Ten, Day Four:
Praying Big and Bold!

Father, help me to believe You to do exceedingly, abundantly beyond anything I can ask or think.

Continuing from yesterday, many years ago, when the kids were two and four, I had a passion I believe was God inspired to pray for every public school in the state of Texas. This seemed like an insurmountable task. I would wake up at 5:30 every morning, and I would take a map of Texas counties, (yes, a paper map, remember those?) get online, and go through one school district at a time. I would pray for the principal, vice principal, and any other name listed, and I would pray God's protection over the school. Anyone who knows me would assume I prayed for the salvation of every child to walk through those doors, and I did. Many things were asked of my amazing God at that little table in our Texas bedroom. In less than a year, the task was completed. I will never see if there was some huge answer to those prayers or only a few. But I trust in my God enough to know my heart did that for a reason, even if the reason was to teach me obedience without need for reward.

Jesus was amazed at the faith of the centurion in Luke 7:8–10 who believed Him to heal his servant without needing His presence. Luke actually uses the word "marveled," that Jesus marveled at his faith. Remember from earlier in the study from the book of John when Jesus showed Thomas the scars after the resurrection. "Jesus said to him, 'Have you believed because you have seen me? Blessed are those who have not seen and yet have believed'" (John 20:29).

Though these people had the amazing gift of asking Jesus in person, we have the gift of asking Him also. We ask in prayer. But seeing the repetition of Jesus' words, "according to your faith," shows us that our belief matters. Where we ask is in prayer. Where we believe is in our hearts. I want to be like that centurion who caused Jesus to marvel at his faith. Don't you? Let's boldly pray "exceedingly, abundantly beyond what we can ask or think" from a God we believe!

What could you ask God that would be bigger than what you would imagine to ask Him?

What are the desires of your heart you don't really believe He will do so you don't ask?

Ask Him for one thing that would be for God's glory that You don't think would ever happen. Be specific and direct. Write it out!

A Call to Prayer

Friend, you have released prayer's power by imitating Jesus' authenticity and recognizing His divinity.

I have no idea how little Mrs. Lucy Mebane cajoled my nineteen-year-old self into committing to pray an hour every single week in that cramped dingy space at First Baptist Church in Waco, Texas. Twenty-eight years later, tears stream down my face recognizing how much I would have missed out on had I not shown up that day. Every part of me screamed, "You don't want to do this! Pray for an hour, every week? You don't have time. What is that going to accomplish?"

Little did I know it would inspire me, comfort me, change my heart, my actions, my life, and my relationship to God forever.

"Father, give precious Lucy in heaven a big thank you for me! Amen!"

I want to thank you for sticking with me to the end. For those of us who spend time with Him, we understand it is an adventure. From my limited experience, prayer has enhanced my life journey repeatedly. Sometimes I sit in silence with Him. Sometimes His message screams. Sometimes He pricks my heart. Sometimes He teaches me truth. Sometimes He comforts, and sometimes He directs. But He is always there. Friends are great, but having the One who spoke the stars into being walk me through life is a friendship unspeakably beyond anything I could have anticipated!

Wherever you started in your journey of prayer, I hope you are experiencing Him in this way. If we learn about prayer, but never pray, how foolish!

Let's remember Jesus made the way for us to pray! He gave us this privilege and wants us to enjoy all the benefits.

We talked quite a bit about prayer being a commitment. It will not happen without us choosing to invest time to talk to God and deepen our relationship with Him. Whatever time we set aside to grow the relationships in our lives, let's choose daily to prioritize our God this same way.

There are so many parts of prayer we did not cover, and if you want to delve into that more, there are countless great books on prayer. Reading about prayer teaches us so much, but actually praying teaches even more. "Pray without ceasing" as the apostle Paul put it.

Please take some time right now to review the concepts God has been working you through. Flip through the book to places where something caught your heart, then journal what specifics you have learned and how you can continue them in your life.

Praying is not something you do for a season, then transition to the next latest and greatest thing. Praying remains needed for our entire lifetime. When I choose to not pray, unrest looms in my soul from the absence of a God conversation. How wise we are when we grab the peace that surpasses all understanding by maintaining a conversation with the Prince of Peace!

www.ingramcontent.com/pod-product-compliance
Lightning Source LLC
Chambersburg PA
CBHW062101090426
42741CB00015B/3298